EQUIPMENT LEASING PARTNERSHIPS

A Complete Investment Guide to the Economics, the Risks and the Opportunities

PARTNERSHIPS

E.F. Cudworth

PROBUS PUBLISHING COMPANY
Chicago, Illinois

This publication is designed to provide accurate and authoritative information in regard to the subject matter covered. It is sold with the understanding that the publisher is not engaged in rendering legal, accounting or other professional service.

Library of Congress Cataloging-in-Publication Data

Cudworth, E. F.
    Investment guide to leasing partnerships / E. F. Cudworth.
        p.   cm.
    Includes index.
    ISBN 1-55738-088-0
    1. Industrial equipment leases—United States.   2. Investments—United States.   3. Partnership—United States.   I. Title
    HD39.4.C83   1989
    332.63—dc20   89-32957
                                                       CIP

Printed in the United States of America

1   2   3   4   5   6   7   8   9   0

Contents

Part IV Resources

Index

I
Leasing as an Investment

1
Overview

Equipment leasing was first used in Mesopotamia and Egypt. Archaeological records show that temple priests leased agricultural tools to farmers. Ancient kingdoms of Babylonia, Phoenicia, Greece, and Rome were also known to lease both real and personal property. The decision to lease or buy has always been based on which method of financing made more economic sense for the user of the equipment.

In business schools this situation is commonly referred to as the *lease versus buy decision.* The fundamental principle that underlies leasing is that ownership of an asset is just one way to make use of that asset but what is crucial is how that asset is used and financed.

From an historical view, equipment leasing did not come into wide use (aside from some capital-intensive industries such as transportation) until the late 1960s even though it appears that the earliest recorded use of equipment leasing was in about 2000 B.C. in the Mespotamian city of Ur. Until the Industrial Revolution created an immensely larger production and economic system, there was very little demand for equipment leasing. At first equipment leasing was used in the financing of ships and railroads. Legal prohibitions to the leasing of personal property were found in English common law until the ninteenth century.

This changed when a small automobile maker in the 1920s decided he needed to do something dramatic to sell cars. That automaker was Alfred Sloan of General Motors, the founder of the modern corporation. Sloan extended credit to customers so that they would be able to purchase his cars.

The decision to sell cars on credit began the process in America toward a wider understanding of the more productive use of money to acquire equipment—which is what equipment leasing is about. During the past 50 years equipment leasing has become a major force in the financing of U.S. business.

Equipment leasing is financed by several types of leasing companies, including bank holding companies or their subsidiaries, independent leasing companies, so-called captive subsidiaries of nonfinancial firms, divisions of insurance companies, and investment bankers. These different types of leasing firms are primarily defined by the sources of capital used to finance their leasing activities. The methods used in engaging in leasing transactions are essentially the same. Independent leasing companies obtain their original funds from banks and other sources to focus on specialized leasing activities. Leasing brokers, which form another part of the industry, mainly serve as intermediaries between the lessor and lessee. Commercial banks, investment banks, and smaller independent leasing companies often assume the role of leasing broker.

Leasing Funds Emerge

In the mid-1970s leasing operators found a new means of funding—*limited partnerships*. Developed first in the oil and gas industry, this capital-raising vehicle spread rapidly into the real estate business. Limited partnerships provided attractive tax shelters for a new average investor market. These direct participation financial investments grew rapidly but equipment leasing remained relatively small until the mid-1980s.

The problem with leasing partnerships for the investor was that they simply could not create the high write-off financial structures which tax law permitted in real estate and oil and gas. Congress was starting to nip away at all tax shelters as early as the late 1970s. By 1986 the U.S. Tax Reform Act changed the rules of passive loss deductions and virtually eliminated the demand for limited partnership shelters. New tax laws have emerged that tend to place the economics of an investment above the tax consequences of the investment decision.

Growth of Equipment Leasing

With this process of tax reform, the limited partnership business—which by 1986 had become a $13 billion a year investment business—shifted emphasis from sheltered investment vehicles to current income types of investments, cash-on-cash sorts of investments where investors primarily sought quarterly cash distributions. The result has been a dramatic increase in the sale of equipment leasing partnerships.

Figure 1.1 shows that public equipment leasing fund sales jumped about four-fold to roughly $800 million in 1986 from just five years earlier. In 1987, this figure increased to about $1.1 billion, and according to industry estimates, the equipment leasing public funds market was expected to hit about $1.2 billion in 1988—still growing, although more slowly, but all the more noteworthy because other types of partnership sales have plunged during the same period. In the past five years, the equipment leasing public funds market has grown at about a 30 percent annual rate.

As an investment vehicle, equipment leasing partnerships have ample room for future growth. For example, equipment leasing partnerships account for just 6 percent of annual funds raised through direct participation investments (see Figure 1.3). Funds raised from equipment leasing partnerships are about one to two percent of the annual U.S. leasing industry, which the American Association of Equipment Lessors (AAEL) estimated at $100 billion in 1988.

The U.S. leasing industry has grown dramatically in recent years. According to the AAEL, since 1978, leasing has grown over twice as fast as equipment purchases. In 1978, equipment leasing represented about $22.3 billion of the total $178.0 billion U.S. investment in equipment, or about 12.5 percent. By 1988, all U.S. leasing will reach about $99.8 billion of a total equipment investment by American business of $328.8 billion, or a 30.3 percent share. This means that growing share of American business capital is financed through leasing. The primary equipment components of this U.S. leasing market in 1986 were transportation, 32 percent; office and communications, 26 percent; agriculture, medical and industrial

Figure 1.1
Equipment Leasing Partnership Sales

$ Million

Year	Value
1981	200
1982	241
1983	386
1984	478
1985	550
1986	812
1987	1100
1988	1200

Figure 1.2
Additional U.S. Leasing Activity by Equipment Sector, 1986
(in $ billions)

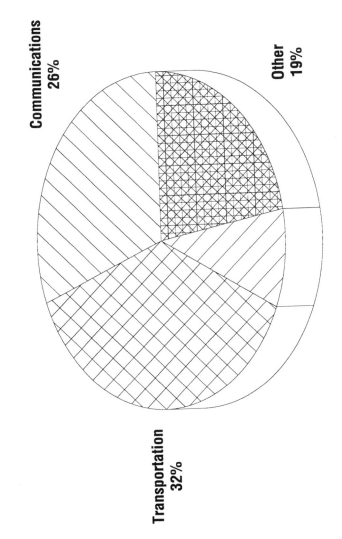

Communications
26%

Other
19%

Agricultural
8%

Transportation
32%

Source: AAEL

Figure 1.3
Direct Participation Market

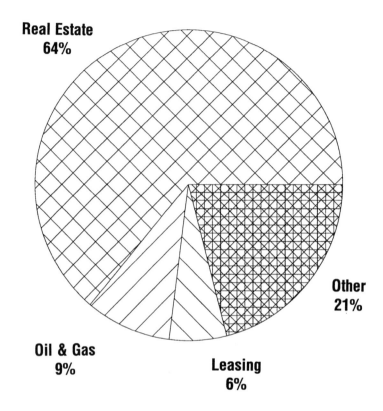

Real Estate
64%

Other
21%

Oil & Gas
9%

Leasing
6%

machinery, 8 percent; and other, about 19 percent (see Figure 1.2).

From an investor's viewpoint, two trends have emerged for equipment leasing partnerships. First, the overall use of leasing by the U.S. (and other major industrial nations) is prominent and still growing. Second, tax laws affecting the limited partnership business have made alternative investments, such as real estate and oil and gas partnerships, less attractive to average investors because of the loss of tax advantages.

Along with these two trends, the leasing industry is consolidating. The combination of deregulation, tax reform, and various accounting changes in recent years has led to an unprecedented number of mergers and acquisitions in the leasing industry. The breakup of AT&T, as one example, has opened up the telecommunications market to leasing, through the regional telephone companies and other independent lessors. While in some cases major corporations may have moved away from tax-oriented leasing, the nature of the leasing industry favors the growth of the leasing partnership funds. The reason is risk versus reward.

The major lessors, typically the banks, are very risk averse. Simply put, these institutions are content to dominate in what is called the *finance lease* or *full-payout lease* where typically the lease provides for the full recovery of the equipment value during the life of the lease term. These are price competitive leases where the advantage is to the banks with the most capital. But these direct financing leases also provide lower returns than other leasing transactions. These aspects will be discussed in more detail in chapters 2 and 3, but for now, the consideration is that public leasing funds are best adapted to relatively riskier lease transactions where most banks fear to tread. These types of leases—operating leases—make sense for many lessees and lessors and provide for greater returns to the investor. This segment of the leasing market continues to grow at a much faster pace and favors the smaller lease operator over the institutional lessor, because of the increasing need for equipment specialization and service.

Public leasing funds have typically focused on those types of equipment and operating leases which better fit the niche of the independent operator. Often this type of leasing operation has looked primarily at high tech sorts of equipment, such as computers or aircraft, which provide higher relative risks but higher rewards too. While this pattern is changing somewhat, the fundamentals of public leasing funds adhere to these broad criteria for the average investor:

- Relatively high cash yields that surpass the returns of bonds or money market type instruments

- Some reasonable protection of investor capital

> Some way for the "average investor" to have access to a big market like leasing for a relatively small entry, as little as $2,500

Notice that we keep the phrase "average investor" in quotation marks. The reason is simple: there are no average investors. Some investment products match up better with certain types of investors for a variety of reasons, risk and reward being the big factors. But if this book does nothing else, it should demonstrate that equipment leasing partnerships are not, repeat not, for everyone. Unfortunately, as with many other types of investment vehicles, public leasing partnerships have been sold to the wrong people for the wrong reasons.

There is no guarantee that any investment fund is without risk. For example, despite what some leasing fund syndicators may promise through various schemes such as zero-coupon side investments, there are no assurances that a leasing fund will return the investor's initial capital investment.

With leasing funds, the investor must consider the difference between return *on* investment versus return *of* investment. This is discussed in more detail in chapter 5, but any investor or financial service professional must clearly understand that quarterly or annual cash distributions include both income earned from the lease operation *and* the return of capital that is the consequence of equipment depreciation.

Equipment is a depleting asset. Equipment does not appreciate except in the most extraordinary circumstances.

There are also emotional considerations in any investment decision. This may sound foolish, but many leasing funds investors will buy into a particular fund simply because they like the equipment; they like airplanes or computers or what-have-you. We're not saying anything new here about consumer or investor motivation, but no matter how much you like the equipment—the thing itself—the professional investor and financial advisor must sort out one fundamental concept of leasing: equipment, as any other asset, does not automatically make money. It must be operated and managed. The same piece of equipment can make a lot of money for a good operator but prove disastrous in the hands of an inexperienced lessor. General partner know-how is crucial to a fund's success.

Equipment leasing partnership investments are still relatively new investment options. As with any new investment option, it is wise to first understand how these investments work and then how they fit into the general scheme of investments and personal financial strategies.

All limited partnerships provide investors with an opportunity to invest directly into various types of investments. Unlike the purchase of a stock, the buyer of limited partnership units is buying an interest in the management of specific types of assets. As a limited partner, the investor is still able to obtain partial tax shelter (but not passive activity losses). In the case of equipment leasing, the limited partners are able to partially shelter current income distributions through depreciation of the fund's assets. And depending on how the lease is structured, this may permit substantial shelter during the early years of the fund's existence.

But as a practical matter, equipment leasing funds are like any other investment. Namely, they must be managed to produce a profit for the investors. This principle must be absorbed deeply into the financial professional's evaluation of any prospective partnership investment.

The other principle of equipment leasing is that it is a highly specialized sort of business. For investors and advisors two key ingredients must be weighed: first the equipment itself and second how the lease operation is structured. Both ingredients, of course, require experienced and able general partner management.

Types of Leasing Funds

Equipment leasing funds can be classified in just a few ways. There are public and private funds, as with any limited partnership offering. Publicly offered funds require more stringent regulatory compliance. Private funds are intended for more knowledgeable investors and for much higher minimum levels of investment. For the most part, we will concern ourselves with public equipment leasing partnerships. But the principles of good due diligence apply to both classes of leased partnership investment.

Part II details the types of leasing funds available. These leasing funds can be classed by equipment type or by fund structure. The two most popular types of equipment funds in recent years have been computer and aircraft funds, partly because investors and advisors are generally familiar with this type of equipment. Other major classes of equipment leasing partnerships would include other types of transportation equipment, medical and industrial equipment and telecommunications equipment. Leasing funds can also be classified by fund structure. So-called income funds are those that emphasize current income over long-term appreciation. By far, this is the most important type of fund structure since 1986 tax reform. Another type of leasing fund is characterized as a growth fund, where the object is to reinvest substantial portions of lease cash flow into new equipment or an alternative investment so as to provide the return of an investor's initial capital at the end of the program. Lease fund programs are considered fixed investments whose life ranges from 5 to 14 years. Because very few equipment leasing partnerships have gone full-cycle at this writing, it is important to distinguish between fact and promise. So much hinges on the eventual disposition of the leased assets—the residual value—that we will spend a good deal of time evaluating how residual values enter into the economics of evaluating leasing investments.

Relatively new types of equipment leasing partnerships have also emerged. These include venture leasing funds and lease options funds. These types of funds present special characteristics that hinge more on the trading features of the leasing business—than on the somewhat more predictable economics of the equipment itself. For example, in venture leasing funds the general partner and leasing fund operator seek higher lease income from lessees through a combination of rents and equity kickers. In effect, the lease transaction resembles venture capital financing with the potential of home runs as well as strikeouts. These special-purpose leasing funds are treated in chapters 12, 13, and 14.

Lease Analysis

Part III of this book is devoted to techniques for analyzing equipment leasing partnerships. By far the most important ingredient is the ability of the general partner who will manage the fund's assets. As any experienced financial advisor knows, there are no easy ways to quantify the capability of a general partner—but there are ways to evaluate the reasonableness of the general partner's projections and the fund's structure.

Yield analysis is an essential prior factor in any decision to buy a leasing fund. Unfortunately, too many broker/dealers and financial advisors rely too completely on the promises and presumptions of fund syndicators. We encourage a hearty look at the assumptions behind any fund projection. Wherever possible we urge that actual management performance in prior funds be used in any financial projections. Since most investors and financial advisors do not have endless time to do all the due diligence, this book includes tips on how to get the most from broker/dealer due diligence experts and how to quickly spot danger signs.

Overcoming Front-End Loads

As with any limited partnership investment, the investor must deal with high front-end fees, usually 15 percent to 20 percent of investor capital right off the top. The reasons for these relatively high offering and initial management fees are varied. Additionally, general partner management fees and incentive fees comprise significant factors in evaluating ultimate investor yields. Chapter 17 deals with offering terms and management fees.

In Part IV, several resources are given for reference, including a glossary of leasing terms and profiles of leasing fund sponsors. Throughout the book, however, we will try to talk about leasing with a minimum of jargon. The leasing industry is specialized, but it is really not all that difficult to grasp the essentials and separate the hype from substance.

2
How Leasing Works

An *equipment lease* is a contract where one party—the lessor who owns the equipment—conveys use of that equipment to another—the lessee — in exchange for periodic rental payments. Within this broad definition reside a variety of options and types of leases.

Typically, the lessee investigates and decides on a particular piece of equipment. Along with this specific make and model of equipment, the lessee will decide on warranties and delivery and will negotiate the price of the equipment. Once the actual equipment decision is made, the lessee will negotiate with a lessor to determine the terms of the lease, covering length of lease and rental payments. The lessee will assign purchase rights to the lessor after the lease is signed. The equipment is purchased by the lessor according to the lessee's specifications, and delivered to the lessee who accepts the equipment and begins rental payments. The lessee will also choose from among various options once the lease term ends, including to return the equipment to the lessor, purchase the equipment, or to renew the lease.

Lease Types

Two basic types of leases are the finance lease and the operating lease. If ownership of the equipment passes to the lessee at the end of the lease term, the lease payments represent the full value of the equipment and this lease is called a *finance* or *full-payout* type of lease. If the lease does not cover the full value of the equipment's original cost, it is an *operating*, or *non-full-payout lease*.

The three general categories of finance-type leases are non-tax-oriented leases (also known as conditional sales leases), tax-oriented true leases (sometimes called guideline leases) and tax-oriented TRAC leases. In a *conditional sale lease* (known also as a *security agreement*), the lessee has an option to purchase the equipment at a predetermined (usually bargain-basement) price at the expiration of the lease). In this case, the user is considered as the owner of the equipment from the start. The tax-oriented true lease conforms to Internal Revenue Service guidelines to determine the availability of tax benefits to the lessor and the deduction of rental payments by the lessee. *TRAC leases,* short for terminal rental adjustment clause, specify that the lessee assumes all the residual risk of the equipment. This means that the lessee may or may not purchase the equipment at the end of the lease term but at a price to be determined at the fair market value of the equipment at the end of the lease term (i.e, the *residual value* of the equipment).

Tax-oriented leases involve either *direct-financing* or *single-investor leases* for 100 percent financing of the equipment or involve *leveraged leasing* through third-party investors who provide debt funding in addition to the lessor's equity. Leveraged leasing is used especially for big-ticket equipment, such as aircraft, oil rigs, and rail equipment. According to industry estimates, leveraged leasing accounts for as much as one-third of the value of all equipment leases. Direct financing is used primarily for office and computer equipment, motor vehicles, and manufacturing equipment.

While the situation in equipment leasing limited partnerships is changing as the market grows and diversifies into new equipment areas, much of the equipment purchased for partnership portfolios is structured under operating leases. Under an *operating lease,* the lessee acquires use of the equipment for a fraction of the life of an asset. Operating lease terms are usually much shorter than finance leases. And typically, operating leases include provisions for the lessee's separate payment of insurance, maintenance, and servicing of the equipment. In the case where the lessee pays for insurance and maintenance separately, the lease is called a *net lease.* A key feature of operating leases is that the lease obligation does not show on the lessee's balance sheet.

Why Firms Lease

Leasing has always appealed to cash-poor firms which want to avoid big downpayments and seek to stretch out repayment. In addition, leasing is a flexible alternative. Company A can match its equipment cost to optimize not only its cash flow but also to match use of the equipment to the practical life of the equipment.

For example, in the case of computer and specialized production equipment, a company can experience the obsolescence of the equipment either through technology or market changes, long before the equipment actually wears out. The flexibility of an operating lease shifts this risk of high-tech or market obsolescence to the lessor. Additionally, the lessee can avoid the problem of disposing of the equipment himself. Naturally, the lessee pays a premium for these operating lease advantages.

While there are tax advantages to leasing, these advantages have declined under recent tax reform. Significantly, in 1986 Congress eliminated the investment tax credit (ITC), modified depreciation, rules and lowered corporate tax rates. The combination of the loss of these three factors reduced the attraction of tax-oriented leasing. However, new alternative minimum tax (AMT) provisions have had the effect of enhancing tax-oriented leasing among some corporations subject to the AMT under the new law.

The leasing alternative also provides management with fewer financial burdens than might be imposed if the company went through traditional debt financing. Depending on circumstances and the lender, a company may face protective restrictions by the lender, such as minimum working capital requirements, which can often hamstring the operator. Leasing may also be a way to hurdle budget restrictions, for example, barriers that may be imposed on a division or a government agency's capital budget. Off-balance sheet financing, such as leasing usually provides, is a way around such budgeting restrictions.

Lease Program Flexibility

As you can see, the primary advantage of leasing for the lessee is flexibility. Lease transactions can be structured to virtually meet every need imaginable.

For example, in a *custom lease*, lessee cash payments can be adjusted to meet expected cash flow, over a few years or even on a seasonal basis.

Another example is a *master lease program* where the lessee acquires equipment needed immediately but also fixes other basic terms for acquiring other equipment in the future.

A manufacturer may also use leasing to stimulate his own sales and finance his operation under what is termed *vendor leasing programs*. In these cases, the lessor offers leases through the vendor's sales representatives. In effect, the lessor acts as the captive finance firm for the manufacturer or distributor by extending leasing options to customers of the firm.

Sales and leaseback agreements are arrangements where a company will sell equipment it owns to a lessor who will in turn lease back the equipment to the user. Such arrangements free up cash for the equipment user and can provide tax benefits to the lessor.

The flexible options of lease transactions include facility leases, overrun leases, computer leases, fleet leases, and others. In a *facility lease*, the entire facility, including equipment, can be leased. For construction of new plants, this type of arrangement can provide another type of construction financing. An *overrun lease* provides a means of financing cost overruns. In a *computer lease*, the lessee can finance upgrades and enhancements (additional memory, etc.). A *fleet lease* can be customized for operators of large numbers of trucks and other vehicles. The range of leasing options, is limited only by the imagination of those party to the transaction.

Leasing Partnership Structures

A lessor is essentially an investor. He invests in a particular piece of equipment which he rents to a lessee. To be successful, a lessor must obviously know in what and with whom he is investing. In equipment leasing limited partnerships, the lessor is you. You, as the leasing partnership investor, are buying certain assets which you intend to lease through the general partner of the fund, who works for you. This may sound childish but that's what happens. You are essentially betting that the general partner will make money for you by managing your equipment assets.

This distinction is important because in the partnership syndication business, a syndicator may be good at marketing partnership shares but terrible as a leasing operator, and what's worse, you may not know how ineffective your general partner is until years after your original investment has been made. The reason for this is that in almost all leasing transactions, the real profit is not realized until the equipment has gone full-cycle—meaning, the equipment has been managed and remarketed successfully over a long period of time.

Equipment must first be initially leased. This involves the ability to economically compete for equipment and lessees in a very big marketplace. Betting on either equipment or a lessee who does not have a future is the basic initial risk of the lessor. Lease rates are a function of competition and risk. An over-eager lessor can short change his future by leasing at too low a rate to lessees who are not worth the risk. A limited partner's investment that has not been reinvested in equipment is idle money.

In the second phase, the lease must be managed. This means more than waiting for payments to come in. The lessor must keep in touch with both the lessee and the marketplace. Insurance, maintenance, and equipment servicing must be done as well as provided for in the lease agreement. Additionally, the general partner must use lease income to acquire new equipment to protect the overall investment of the limited partnership. This is especially true in operating leases where the partnership portfolio is subject to risks from lessee default and market and technological changes.

Finally, the general partner of a leasing fund must be able to successfully remarket the equipment, either through lease renewals, new leases for the equipment, or in sale of the equipment. Trading knowledge of the equipment is a crucial factor in the long-term success of the general partner's performance.

In the limited partnership business, the syndicator of a fund may have expertise in marketing partnership shares but lack any real experience as a leasing operator. This is why investors, financial advisors, and broker/dealers must evaluate the economics of the fund's assumptions and the track record of the general partner.

As noted in chapter 1, the leasing partnership investor gives away between 15 and 20 percent of his original investment in offering costs. This is a big hurdle that can only be justified by the long term success of the fund, and the long-term success of the fund hinges primarily on the expertise of the fund manager. An investor should not be deceived by initial cash distributions from the fund. Such distributions may or may not indicate that the equipment assets are being managed successfully.

3
Leasing Economics

The decision to lease or buy equipment is a financing choice. Theoretically, the decision should have nothing to do with the equipment itself. Leasing academicians and others have constructed extremely complex models to simulate the lease/buy decision to account for a range of criteria. But the problem with such models is that they do not easily include qualitative factors—such as operational flexibility and liquidity preferences—in the equation.

Leasing has become a significant means of financing new equipment in a number of major industries, particularly in computers, commercial airlines, auto fleets, agriculture, and medical and industrial segments. One survey of United Airlines, TWA, Delta, and American Airlines showed these four top carriers had leased 30 percent of their fleets in 1986.

For our purposes, however, we will assume that leasing provides advantages in liquidity and flexibility for different companies at different times. Indeed, according to industry surveys, leasing is used by 8 of 10 American companies at one time or another. The issue for this book is how leasing economics affect the lessor and the investor in a equipment leasing limited partnership.

A lessor obtains income in two basic ways from ongoing rental payments from the lessee and through remarketing of the equipment. From the lessor's point of view, the sum of cash payments from the lessee must pay for the equipment, cover all operating costs, and compensate the lessor with a profit. As we've stated, equipment leasing partnerships rely primarily on operating types of leases where the lease term covers just a fraction of the original equipment cost.

The remarketing bet becomes that much more important in the economics of the operating lease.

Lease Rate Factors

The key measure of ongoing lease income is called the *lease rate factor* (LRF) which is the net monthly rental payment expressed as a percentage of original equipment cost. For example, an LRF of 3.0 means that the lessor obtains 3.0 percent of the original equipment cost each month, or 36 percent (12×3 percent) each year. This would mean that the lessor needs 34 months to recover the value of the original equipment cost, exclusive of operating costs and profit.

But what accounts for the lease rate in the first place? The first issue, of course, is the equipment itself—its cost, expected practical life, and eventual residual value at the end of the lease term. To illustrate, equipment with a relatively long life and low-obsolescence like intermodal containers will have a relatively high residual value, and thus, all things equal, a lower lease rate. Market availability of the equipment, now and in the future, will also affect the cost of the equipment and its lease value. Conversely, high-tech equipment like telecommunications and most types of personal computers are subject to rapid obsolescence and thus are riskier and command higher lease rates.

Market considerations also influence the alternative cost of financing the equipment for the lessee as well as the lessor. A potential lessee will shop around for the best price. For the lessor, the credit-worthiness of the lessee is important. The worse the credit, the higher the lease rate to compensate the lessor for perceived credit risks. Negotiating lease rates and terms is an art and skill that must be highly developed in the lessor of the equipment.

Lease Terms

Lessors often try to lessen their exposure to credit risks by insisting on commitment fees which are deposits made in advance by the lessee to cover perceived credit risks. This can be as simple as the standard first-and-last month's payment or the deposit of escrow fees approaching 50 percent of original equipment cost to protect the lessor. Net leases, as we've mentioned, are a means where the lessee stipulates that he will pay separately for equipment costs associated with insurance and maintenance. In some cases, under what is called *stipulated loss value* (or insured value of the equipment), a schedule is drawn up which establishes the lessee's liability under the lease at various times in case of equipment loss or damage.

The length of the lease as well as the various lease provisions obviously influence the economics of the lease transactions. The longer the operating lease, for example, the more advantageous it is for the lessor. Renewal lease rates and secondary and tertiary lease rates are crucial to the ongoing cash flow generated by the equipment.

Residual Value

Perhaps the key element in the ultimate success of managing an operating lease is the eventual market value at the end of the lease term. Expected residuals influence the equation of the lease, right through the life of the equipment, not just when that equipment is finally sold by the lessor but throughout its history under lease. And here the economics began to look very murky. The reason is simple: no one can predict with absolute certainty what a piece of equipment will be worth 3, 5, 10 or 20 years into the future.

Residual value assumptions form the very basis for ultimate success of nearly all equipment leasing limited partnership income funds. This is illustrated in Figure 3.1. In this hypothetical case, we can see how different residual value assumptions can dramatically change projected cash flow and annual return on investment.

In Figure 3.1, three limited partnership funds each buy a mainframe computer for $1 million. Each fund puts the equipment on an operating lease for three years at a net monthly lease rate of 2.5 percent of the original equipment cost (deducting such partnership costs as management fees to the general partner, maintenance, insurance, and overhead).

Each leasing partnership fund in our illustration releases the computer in years four and five at 2.5 percent of the equipment's residual value, which in each case is logically less than the original purchase price. During those final two years of the program, the equipment loses one-third of its value. Then the equipment is sold.

The only difference in our three hypothetical programs is the value of the equipment at the end of the initial lease. In the first case, Scenario A, the residual value is 60 percent of the purchase price,

Figure 3.1
Residual Value Impact

Scenario Chart

Scenario	Initial Monthly Lease-Rate	Cash Flow Years 1-3	Initial Residual End Year 3	Re-Lease Monthly Rate	Cash Flow Years 4-5	Residual End Year 5	Cash Flow On Sale	Total Cash Flows	Annual Return
A	2.5%	$900,000	60%	1.5%	$360,000	40%	$400,000	$1,660,000	13.2%
B	2.5%	$900,000	45%	1.13%	$271,200	30%	$300,000	$1,471,200	9.4%
C	2.5%	$900,000	30%	0.75%	$180,000	20%	$200,000	$1,280,000	5.6%

Different residual rates after first three years produce very different results over the life of the equipment. Note how the lower initial residual rate reduces both re-lease rates and gains when the equipment is sold at end of Year 5. While cash flows for each scenario are the same ($900,000) for the first three years, the lower residual rates will force much lower overall returns over the life of the program.

Source: Financial Planning magazine.

which means the second lease brings in 1.5 percent of the original price per month (60 percent of the original value times 2.5 percent equals 1.5 percent).

In the second case, Scenario B, the residual value is somewhat less, 45 percent, and in the third case, Scenario C, lower still at 30 percent. This means that cash flow in years four and five is reduced accordingly in the second and third partnership programs, and ultimate resale values are also reduced.

The result of these differences in residuals is anything but small: cash-on-cash annual returns of 13.2 percent, 9.4 percent and 5.6 percent in Scenarios A, B, and C, respectively.

You may ask if one appraiser's residual assumption would be so far different from another professional appraisal? The answer is that many factors go into a residual value assumption, and some of it is personal opinion. In chapter 5, we'll discuss in more detail how these residual assumptions can be judged as reasonable or not and how to distinguish between return on investment and return of investment.

It is important to understand that the economics of a lease transaction, especially in an operating lease, is influenced dramatically by the assumptions made at the onset. Expected lease rates, assumed residuals, and how the lease is structured influence leasing partnership economics.

Lease Structure

Equipment operating leases have the ability to throw off more cash quickly than other types of partnership investments such as in real estate. Estimates can vary but comparisons between real estate and equipment leasing partnerships indicate that the range of annual cash flow for a real estate partnership is between 5 and 10 percent compared to 20 and 40 percent for an equipment leasing income fund.

One of the tenets, however, of managing operating leases is that the assets be fully used. It is a little like running a grocery store, where the emphasis is on turnover as well as margins. For the lessor, this means equipment must always be producing dollars. Equipment off-lease, that is, equipment that is not profitably leased, produces no income. Cash flow that is not reinvested in new equipment does not build up the fund's portfolio and may shortchange the future of the fund.

Lease operators are managing equipment assets. A limited partnership fund must have a plan to manage those assets for investors over a long period of time. An equipment leasing fund can be structured with various objectives in mind. For example, many equipment leasing funds can opt for depreciation schedules which will shelter a considerable portion of investor cash distributions during the early years. But if an equipment reinvestment plan is not included in the fund's operating structure, what will be left for the investor in the later years of the program? Again, like the retailer, the lessor must continue to turn over equipment assets to maximize the long-term return of the portfolio.

Equipment leasing funds can also be structured with varying amounts of debt, where a fund borrows from a lending source to leverage the amount of equipment purchased for the portfolio. Debt produces various tax and risk implications, depending on the amount of debt obtained. Most income funds, those that stress high current income, avoid much debt because it reduces current income. These high debt, so-called growth funds will be discussed later in chapter 7.

There are other types of lease structures other than operating leases that aim for high current income. One example is typical of the intermodal container leasing industry. In this case, the typical lease structure is so called *master lease programs* between the lessor and major shippers and common carriers. Containers are leased for relatively short periods of time by shippers, for the time needed to move merchandise on ship across the ocean, or inland via rail or truck. In effect, the container leasing business resembles the auto rental business. Higher lease rates are possible because of the convenience and flexibility of delivering the equipment easily as short-term needs arise. The goal for the lessor of container equipment is still the same: to keep his containers on lease, producing high income through effective releasing of the equipment.

Some *full-payout structures* are also able to generate high lease rates. An example would be to lease equipment, say telecommunications devices, under firm full-payout contracts with smaller companies for higher rentals. Here the risk is weighted toward the creditworthiness of the lessee. Depending on the ability of the lessor to carefully pick lessees and protect his investment through various schemes such as upfront deposits and commitments from the lessee, this type of lease structure can also meet the criteria of high cash income for an equipment leasing partnership.

The key economic characteristics of equipment leasing public funds are that they:

- Generate substantial cash flow
- Provide partial shelter through depreciation
- Provide a method to protect investor capital through reinvestment and other means
- Fit an economic niche in the larger world of equipment leasing

On the last point, equipment leasing funds should engage in markets that are not dominated by major traditional financial institutions which can bid down lease rates. Leasing, for the most part, is an institutionally driven marketplace. For leasing limited partnerships to make sense, they must serve markets which the big boys choose to ignore.

Lease Funds Niche

Essentially what we have said is that leasing public funds are best suited to those situations where the element of risk prevents major institutional lessors from bidding down lease rates. We have also indicated that equipment leasing partnerships have a new advantage over real estate partnerships because leasing can generate more cash for investors under the reforms of recent tax law.

For many observers, the most suitable leasing fund niches tend to be in areas where there is:

- Higher credit risk
- Higher residual risk
- Reduced tax orientation

There is also a need for public leasing funds to extend out on a long enough term to amortize the relatively high upfront offering costs and fees.

4

Tax Reform and Equipment Leasing

Tax reform has been a persistent cry for some years. Nearly every session of the U.S. Congress has tinkered with the tax implications of leasing since the late 1970s but no measures were as far-reaching as the Tax Reform Act (TRA) of 1986. And what's even more problematical, there's no assurance that a new session will not change things around this year or the year after. Such is the landscape though and it is useful to understand what the recent changes have wrought and how equipment leasing partnerships have benefited for the present.

TRA '86 reached deep into tax law to unsettle the world of leasing. The major changes brought on for leasing by the new law were:

- Repeal of the investment tax credit

- Elimination of passive losses

- New depreciation rules and schedules

- Lower marginal corporate and personal tax rates

For equipment leasing partnerships, the new tax law provided a strong stimulus, for two basic reasons. First, competing limited partnership investments such as real estate (which had dominated the field of direct participation investments) fared worse than equipment leasing. In effect, the field of play evened up a bit. Second, the new tax regime made the economics of an investment more decisive because heavy tax writeoffs were reduced. This second point has encouraged investors to look for income-oriented products such as equipment leasing.

Even before the advent of tax reform, leasing partnerships were ascendant in the marketplace. For the past five years, leasing partnerships have drawn increasing numbers of investors and dollars. Some of this may be explained by the increased exposure of leasing partnerships in the financial services marketplace, that is, more leasing sponsors entering the field, increased sales effort by sponsors, broker dealers, and financial advisors and just the growing awareness of a new investment vehicle by investors.

Add to this history cyclical downturns in oil and gas and real estate, and one can see investors drilling for new investments in the equipment leasing arena.

Equipment leasing benefited over real estate in a major instance because of the changes involving capital gains treatment. Previous to TRA 86, real estate investors were taxed on the difference between a property's appreciated price at sale and the depreciated basis at capital gains rates—which essentially meant that 60 percent of the profit was excluded from taxation. But now that capital gains and ordinary income gains are taxed at the same rate, ordinary income from equipment leasing earns the same treatment as capital gains. A plus for equipment leasing.

In addition, real estate depreciation schedules have become less generous. Commercial real estate must now be written off over 31.5 years on a straightline depreciable basis (contrasted with 19 years before TRA 86). Equipment leasing fares much better on changes in depreciation rules.

Some categories of equipment lost a little on depreciation, but other equipment items gained a little. Manufacturing equipment must be written off more slowly (seven years versus five years) but the applicable accelerated depreciation was liberalized. Similar changes left the field of equipment depreciation relatively intact, which provides a benefit considering all the other tax advantages that were trimmed by the new reforms. (Figure 4.1 gives a partial list of how different equipment is treated under the current tax law.)

Alternative Minimum Tax

TRA 86 also mandated new rules concerning alternative minimum tax (AMT) for corporations. In effect many corporations, depending

Figure 4.1
Major Equipment Depreciation Schedules
Under Tax Reform Act of 1986

Equipment Category	Depreciation Method	Recovery Years
Automobiles	200%	5
Business Aircraft	200	7
Commercial Aircraft	200	7
Computers, mainframe	200	5
Computer disk drives	200	5
Co-generation	150	15
CAT scanners	200	5
Construction equipment	200	5
Container, ship	150	15
Container, truck	200	5
Fiber optic lines	150	15
Hospital equipment	200	5
Manufacturing	200	7
Mining equipment	200	7
Oil refinery	200	10
Land drill rigs	200	5
Railcar containers	200	7
Satellite communications	200	5
Telephone switching	200	5

Note: TRA 86 established eight rather than five classes of ACRS (Accelerated Cost Recovery System) as was true under prior law. For the four categories under 10 years of recovery (3, 5, 7 and 10 years), the 200% double declining balance method of depreciation can be used. For the 15 and 20 year ACRS equipment categories, the 150 percent double declining balance method can be used. Straightline methods are required for residential and commercial real estate with 27.5 and 31.5 depreciable lives.

on their individual tax situation, may be subject to the new minimum tax that arises out of discrepancies between reported income and book value. In many cases, the impact of the new AMT has shifted the decision in favor of corporate leasing over a purchase of equipment.

Figure 4.2 gives an illustration of how AMT benefits leasing in general. The heart of the issue is that many corporations can avoid higher taxes under the new AMT system if they choose to lease. It is difficult to judge just how much the new AMT rules have benefited leasing, but most industry observers say the long-term effect will be positive for equipment leasing.

Figure 4.2
Impact of the AMT on an Equipment Purchase vs. Leasing

	EQUIPMENT PURCHASED		EQUIPMENT LEASED	
	Regular Tax System	AMT System	Regular Tax System	AMT System
Net Revenues	$350,000	$350,000	$350,000	$350,000
Interest Expense	(70,000)	(70,000)	—	—
Equip. Rental Expense	—	—	(262,000)	(262,000)
Accelerated Depreciation	(200,000)	(200,000)	—	—
Regular Taxable Income	80,000	80,000	88,000	88,000
Adjustment Items	—	75,000	—	—
AMT Income	—	155,000	—	88,000
Tax Rate	34%	20%	34%	20%
Tax	$ 27,200	$ 31,000	$ 29,920	$ 17,600

Source: American Association of Equipment Lessors

Loss of Investment Tax Credit

By far the biggest overall hit on leasing was the loss of the investment tax credit (ITC), which ranged from 6 to 10 percent under the old law. But interestingly enough, equipment leasing partnerships benefited from this ITC loss. The ITC provided extra tax incentives that could be passed along to the lessee by the lessor in the form of lower initial lease rates. The ITC benefited tax-oriented leasing that is dominated by the major financial institutions. The loss of ITC raised effective lease rates which tended to reduce the overall level of leasing, but it improved the economic niche of leasing partnerships, especially for used equipment.

For example, lease rates for used equipment rose along with new equipment lease rates after the ITC was cut. This enabled lease renewal and release rates to strengthen because the alternative of buying or leasing new equipment was relatively more expensive. Leasing of used equipment became much more attractive to independent lessors because the difference between acquisition cost of the equipment and the level of leases rates improved.

Passive Loss Limitations

Passive loss limitations provided a temporary boon to equipment leasing partnerships because of transition rules which permitted many investors to phase-in their losses from 1987 to 1991. Figure 4.3 provides an analysis of how passive losses from earlier investments could be offset by passive income generated by investing in an equipment leasing partnership. But this was a transitory benefit to leasing partnerships. Of more enduring value is that the elimination of passive losses have encouraged greater interest in low leverage income-oriented investments such as equipment leasing partnerships can offer.

Lower Marginal Tax Rates

Marginal tax rates are always prime political fodder, but the impact of TRA 86 on tax rates was substantial. Individual leasing partnership investors gained on institutional lessors under the new law. Under the old law, individuals had a 4 percent marginal rate disadvantage compared to corporate lessors (50 percent top tax rate versus 46 percent). With the new law, the marginal tax rate for individuals improved to a 6 percent advantage over institutional lessors (28 percent top tax rate for individuals versus 34 percent for institutions).

Fewer Leveraged Funds

The new tax law discourages the use of significant levels of debt in leasing partnerships for the simple reason that highly leveraged equipment funds generate less cash income. Without the ability to write off the passive losses obtained through highly leveraged funds, investors and financial advisors opt for high current income.

The vast majority of today's equipment leasing funds use zero debt in the acquisition of equipment portfolios. This is not to say that no debt is all good because some lower level of debt is useful in building up the assets of the partnership, but most observers of income funds suggest leasing funds should not use more than 20

Figure 4.3
Analysis of Passive Loss Utilization

	Original Shelter		After Tax Reform		
Year	Passive Losses	Phase In	Usable Passive Losses	Current Suspended Losses	Cumulative Suspended Losses
1987	(24,288)	35%	(15,787)	(8,501)	(8,501)
1988	(22,140)	60%	(8,856)	(13,284)	(21,785)
1989	(19,694)	80%	(3,939)	(15,755)	(37,540)
1990	(16,161)	90%	(1,616)	(14,545)	(52,085)
1991	(11,253)	100%	0	(11,253)	(63,338)
1992	0	100%	0	0	(63,338)
1993	0	100%	0	0	(63,338)
1994	0	100%	0	0	(63,338)
1995	0	100%	0	0	(63,338)
1996	0	100%	0	0	(63,338)
	(93,536)		(30,198)		

Figure 4.3
Analysis of Passive Loss Utilization
(continued)

Original Shelter with Leasing Program After Tax Reform

Year	Projected Leasing Cash Flow	Projected Passive Inc. from Leasing	Net Passive Activity	Usable Passive Losses	Current Suspended Losses	Cumulative Suspended Losses	Amount Cum Suspended Losses Used	Gain in Usable Passive Losses
1987	7,500	3,750	(20,538)	(17,100)	(7,188)	(7,188)	0	1,313
1988	7,500	3,750	(18,390)	(11,106)	(11,034)	(18,222)	0	2,250
1989	7,750	3,875	(15,819)	(7,039)	(12,655)	(30,878)	0	3,100
1990	7,750	3,875	(12,286)	(5,104)	(11,057)	(41,935)	0	3,488
1991	8,000	4,000	(7,253)	(4,000)	(7,253)	(49,188)	0	4,000
1992	9,500	4,750	4,750	(4,750)	0	(44,438)	(4,750)	4,750
1993	10,000	5,000	5,000	(5,000)	0	(39,438)	(5,000)	5,000
1994	8,500	4,250	4,250	(4,250)	0	(35,188)	(4,250)	4,250
1995	7,500	3,750	3,750	(3,750)	0	(31,438)	(3,750)	3,750
1996	10,500	5,250	5,250	(5,250)	0	(26,188)	(5,250)	5,250
				(67,348)				37,150

Hypothetical $50,000 leasing investment

Source: *Financial Planning* magazine.

percent debt. (More on this topic in chapters 6 and 7 when we discuss how income funds and so-called growth funds are structured.)

On balance, TRA 86 was a benefit to equipment leasing funds. Of far more consequence to financial professionals is the individual tax circumstance of the investor. The economics of a leasing fund override the tax structure of the offering. One of the advantages of limited partnerships is that they can be divided up for different classes of investors. For example, some fund sponsors may provide different types of partnership units with different objectives and characteristics. In some cases, partnership units can be divided into income units or equity or debt units where different benefits can accrue to different types of investors. These hybrid partnership forms will be discussed in chapter 14.

The real issue for any financial professional and investor is to sort out the chaff from the wheat among competing investments. This is the business of weighing risks against projected returns. Equipment leasing partnerships have unique operating aspects which need to be understood before investing your money.

5
Risks and Returns

The riskiness of any investment, including equipment leasing partnerships, is not incidental. Projected returns, while possible, are not real until the check clears. This sort of skepticism is suggested for any financial advisor and investor when looking at any investment, but especially in equipment leasing investments where the economics are somewhat different because of the depleting nature of equipment assets.

This chapter will review all the areas of risk within a leasing partnership investment but especially the peculiar nature of residual risk. In particular, we want to clarify that cash distributions from a leasing fund represent both earned income and the return of a portion of the investor's capital. The distinction between return on capital and return of capital is an issue to be understood before choosing to invest in a leasing partnership, because it substantially influences real internal rates of return.

The litany of risks inherent in a leasing partnership should explain why returns must be significant to attract an investor. The three principle areas of leasing partnership risk are the equipment leasing business itself, fund management, and creditor and market risks.

General Business Risks

Equipment leasing is a highly competitive business that is subject to a host of pitfalls, including credit losses, equipment obsolescence due to technology and market factors, viability of equipment manufacturers, aggressive competition for leases and equipment, future supply and demand for the equipment, and overall economic conditions.

One leasing sponsor concedes that "no combination of management ability, experience, knowledge, care, or scientific approach can avoid the inherent possibilities of loss arising from one or more" of the equipment risk factors cited earlier. This is a standard disclaimer, of course, but readers should understand that risks are very real in the leasing business. The aim should be to understand the risks and make a realistic judgment on likely returns. To avoid the risk entirely is to avoid all opportunities. We are just suggesting a better knowledge of equipment leasing fund risks.

Some more common types of risks associated with equipment leasing funds include:

Operating Leases.   These usually short-term leases predominate among leasing partnerships. These types of leases produce rents which cover just a portion of the original equipment cost and thus bet on the residual value of the equipment at the end of the lease term. The fund general partner must be able to either renew this lease, release the equipment, or sell the equipment economically at the end of the initial lease—none of which is guaranteed.

Competition.   Leasing partnership managers compete for equipment and lessees in a very aggressive marketplace. Let's take the computer marketplace, which is very popular for leasing funds— some 75 percent of new public leasing funds in 1988 invested primarily in computers and peripheral equipment. The leasing fund general partner is competing against a vast group of full-payout lessors (mostly the banks and major leasing subsidiaries of traditional lending sources), computer manufacturers like IBM (which dwarfs the other computer makers), and the whole universe of independent lessors and even other leasing partnerships.

Residual Risk.   The continuing and future value of the leasing partnership's equipment is dependent on many factors, many of which are out of its control, including equipment quality, timing of acquisition and disposal, demand for used equipment versus costs of new equipment, technological and market obsolescence, and general economic and existing tax conditions.

Lessee Credit Risk.   Defaults are a cost of doing business, but a high rate of default can wreck the performance of any leasing operator. A good rule of thumb used in equipment leasing is that a default rate among lessees should not exceed 2 to 3 percent of the operator's portfolio. If it does, then something's wrong, either with choice of creditors or equipment or both. Of course, a leasing operator can find ways to reduce credit risks by requiring lease commitment fees or escrow deposits.

Leverage Risk.   Leasing portfolio debt creates risk in a couple of ways. Debt interest payments reduce the level of cash distributed to partners. If these debt repayments are not made to lenders, then the partnership faces the possible loss of equity acquired through the loans. Depending on the equipment loan provisions, the assets of the partnership may be subject to cross-collateralization of other program assets and such loan covenants may also affect the releasing and remarketing of equipment beyond the expiration of the lease term. In addition, such debt is usually subject to floating rate adjustments pegged to prime interest rates, in which case, rises in the cost of money will increase the cost of the debt to limited partners. Sometimes, partnerships may also contract debt using balloon payments, relying on its ability to refinance this kind of debt in the future. But such balloon financing also incurs a greater risk too, because the refinancing may not be available or may be available only at sharply higher interest rates.

Regulatory Risk.   In some cases equipment owned by the partnership may be adversely affected by government regulation. A prime example is in the area of transportation equipment, such as aircraft. In recent years, the Federal Aviation Administration has proposed new noise rules for existing commercial aircraft which will dramatically decrease the market value of some types of jet airplanes that will require extensive engine replacement or other noise modification costs to remain flying at major U.S. airports in the upcoming years.

Unspecified Equipment and Unknown Lessee Risks. For the most part leasing funds do not completely specify which equipment and which lessees will acquire the assets to be purchased from fund investment proceeds. The investor and financial advisor will not be assured of the precise equipment to be acquired and to whom it will be leased. There is also the coincident risk that the equipment will not be purchased until a considerable period after the investment has been made. Depending on its ability to find creditworthy lessees and equipment at the right price, a fund may wait for two or even three years to completely invest all investor proceeds. Such delays reduce overall investor returns. A good measure of asset performance is the percentage of equipment assets under lease at any time. Normally, a 95 percent on-lease record is considered a minimum standard. At the startup of a fund, the partnership should acquire all or most all of its assets within the first year after the offering has closed.

Diversification Risks. An equipment portfolio that puts all its investment into one specific type of equipment runs greater risks than one than diversifies its portfolio. A mix of equipment types and industrial applications improves the risks of equipment investment.

Joint Venture Risks. Very often, an equipment leasing fund will enter into joint ventures to acquire new equipment with the general partner or its affiliates and with other limited partnerships that may be managed by the fund's general partner. Such ventures also raise the specter of conflicts of interest which can not be easily measured. For example, the general partner or one of its affiliates may on its own account sell certain equipment to a partnership it also manages. While the general partner has a fiduciary relationship to the limited partnership, this does not always mean that the general partner acts with utter selflessness. Also, the possibility of a default or bankruptcy by any of the other parties to a joint venture will adversely affect the limited partnership's ability to secure the equipment free and clear of other creditor claims.

Illiquid Investment Risk. For the most part, limited partners can not easily get out of their fixed partnership investment. In some cases, the general partner may agree to repurchase limited partner unit shares but often only at a sharp discount. In some cases, a secondary market may have developed for limited partnership shares, but again, this will likely incur a heavy discount for getting out of the partnership. In a few cases, some partnerships have set up mechanisms to trade partnership shares through a master limited partnership (MLP) or by a onetime fund rollup arrangement, but at this writing, such MLPs face IRS treatment as a taxable corporate entity, and limited partners have no assurance of a future public market for fund units. For the most part, an investor is stuck with his leasing partnership investment.

A limited partner has very little recourse if the partnership is doing poorly. As described earlier, the limited partner can try to unload his partnership units by selling them to the general partner or through a secondary market established by a network of broker/dealers, but this is usually done at a hefty discount off the investor's original investment. As with nearly all limited partnerships, there is no public market for the trading of equipment leasing partnership units. It should be clear that these are fixed, illiquid types of investments. With the exception of master limited partnerships, described in chapter 14, the limited partner has no easy way to get out of the fixed investment. There is always litigation, but this is expensive and time-consuming and not a realistic option for most investors.

Tax Risks.   An investor and financial planner make assumptions about a limited partnership whose life may extend 10 to 15 years into the future. With the recent history of tax legislation, there is no assurance that assumptions about tax liability made today will resemble the future tax environment. For example, while it is unlikely, the U.S. Congress may decide that limited partnerships should be treated as associations or corporations for tax purposes, in which case, the partnership will be subject to the same double taxation that affects corporations. The government may also change all the rules again for equipment leasing tax treatment and for methods of partner income allocations. As you can see, such changes can also dramatically influence future returns.

Management Risk.   There is no greater risk to the investor than the abilities and know-how of the fund's general partner. Management effectiveness means good people and a good track record. Even so, there are no guarantees of future success. New management, for example, can be riding on the back of past management which has left the company. Fund managers may have experience in one type of equipment but not another.

Residual Risk Dynamics

The residual bet is what makes or breaks any leasing investment. That's a pretty sweeping assertion, but that is the nature of the leasing partnership business, because of the reliance on operating leases and high-tech equipment such as computers which proliferate among the leasing funds.

From an investment point of view, future cash projections are heavily contingent on residual value assumptions. Because equipment is a depleting asset, the ultimate return is skewed substantially by the result of future residual values, both on the final sale and disposition of the equipment but throughout the ongoing leasing operation in the form of lease renewals and releases.

Quarterly cash distributions include both income earned and a return of capital. If we look at a simple case such as one computer lease, we'll understand why this is obviously a crucial factor in arriving at true returns. Let's say we lease a personal computer bought today for $10,000 for two years at a net monthly lease rate of 3 percent. We release that equipment for another two years at a release rate of 2 percent a month. In the fifth year, we lease the equipment for a final 12 months at a net monthly lease rate of 1 percent and then we sell the computer at the end of year five for $1,500. Cash flow to us would be:

Year
1      $3,600 (3% × 12 × 10,000)
2   3,600
3   2,400 (2% × 12 × 10,000)
4   2,400
5   1,800 (1% × 12 × 10,000) + $1,500 on sale

Total cash return = $15,300

So, we could say that our profit on this equipment was $5,300. Our annual rate of return as follows: 5,300/5 = 1,060 or 1,060/10,000

= 10.6 percent. Ignoring present value considerations to simplify the point, our return of capital and return on capital would be:

Year	Return of Capital	Return on Capital
1	2,540	1,060
2	2,540	1,060
3	1,340	1,060
4	1,340	1,060
5	740 + 1,500 = 2,240	1,060

Figure 5.1 shows how much of the cash distributed is composed of recovery of investment and how much is earned income. The numbers are not especially important in our illustration. What is important is that the graph demonstrates the basic principle of equipment leasing investments. Most of the cash distributions in the early years represent recovery of investment. We can also see that much of the total return of the investment is dependent on the resale of the equipment at the end of the lease.

Figure 5.1 also illustrates the significance of remarketing the equipment in subsequent release or renewal, which is also a function of residual values. Of course, there are various ways to evaluate leasing investment yields using present value reinvestment rates, internal rates of return and payback periods but all we hope to clearly demonstrate at this stage is the substantial influence of residual assumptions on projected real rates of return and why investors must be wary of initial cash distribution assumptions without clearly understanding the likelihood of future release and remarketing of the equipment.

Minimizing Risk = Maximizing Returns

Only through conservative assumptions, particularly in residual value projections, can financial professionals come up with realistic expectations about the likely performance of an equipment leasing partnership.

Equipment leasing is not a plain form of investment. It does involves risk as well as possible rewards. As a fixed income investment, it has certain economic characteristics. Understanding these characteristics will permit better evaluation of product offering claims. Not all leasing partnerships are of the same risk level.

Figure 5.1
Return of Investment versus Earned Income
(in equipment leasing investment)

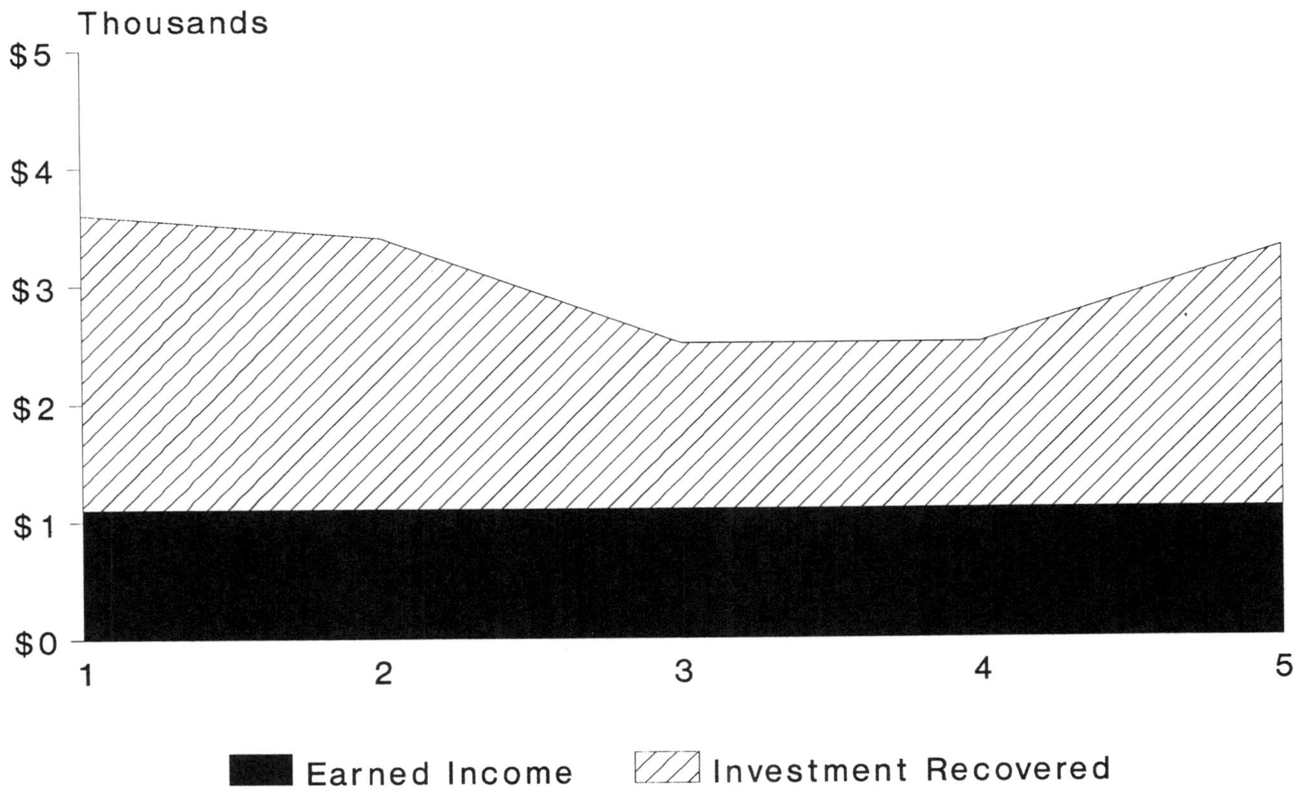

Thousands

Earned Income

Investment Recovered

II
Types of Leasing Funds

6
Equipment Leasing Income Funds

The term *income funds* as used in equipment leasing limited partnerships means that the fund's primary objective is to generate high current income. The stress is on obtaining cash-on-cash returns, some tax shelter for investor cash distributions, and in preserving investor capital contributions. Beyond this description, there really is not a comprehensive definition of a leasing income fund.

The use of so-called leasing income funds came into play in the mid-1970s when a few partnership sponsors began to structure these investment products to take advantage of the cash generating abilities of operating lease activities. Until the mid-1980s, when tax reform seemed likely, most equipment leasing funds mimicked high-writeoff siblings among real estate and oil and gas partnerships.

And the primary means for generating those 4:1 and 5:1 early writeoffs in equipment leasing was the use of debt and lease structures that sought shelter over current income.

Income Fund Operating Characteristics

It used to be that the sole method of structuring an equipment leasing income fund was to invest and manage computer peripheral equipment under short-term operating leases. This is still largely true, but not universal among leasing partnerships. The trend among all leasing funds is toward different types of equipment that are aggressively managed for high current income.

The type of equipment, terms of the lease structure, remarketing ability, credit policy, and reinvestment strategy mainly determine the cash flow characteristics of a leasing income fund. One of the undervalued truths about income funds is that they must be aggressively managed. For example, in a typical leasing computer fund, a given piece of computer peripheral equipment must be leased and renewed or released three of four times to begin to be profitable for the leasing operator. With each renewal or release that equipment must be profitably placed with creditworthy lessees at lease rates that make economic sense. In addition, proceeds from the equipment must be reinvested in new equipment to increase long-term yields and preserve investor capital over fund program lives of between 5 and 15 years.

Equipment Factors

By far the most important factor in successfully operating a leasing income fund is the choice and management of the equipment in the fund's portfolio.

Figure 6.1 provides an inventory of major types of equipment that is typically acquired for leasing funds. Each type of equipment has certain industry and market norms for types of lease, lease terms, residual value assumptions, lease rates, and recovery periods.

Commercial aircraft is one of the most popular types of equipment managed in equipment leasing partnerships. One 1987 estimate showed that almost 40 percent of all dollars invested in leasing partnerships that year were for aircraft programs. New equipment is primarily leased on full-payout leases with terms ranging from 8 to 20 years. For the most part, new commercial jet transport is leased through direct lenders and not leasing partnerships. The reasons are twofold. First, partnerships do not have access to the kind of money involved. (A new Boeing 747 starts at $120 million per copy.) But second, there is not enough yield in these full-payout aircraft leases to satisfy the partnerships.

Used aircraft is somewhat different. Used aircraft commands higher lease rates on short-term operating leases, and there is a substantial market for used aircraft among the many airline startups that have been spawned since the deregulation of the U.S. air transport industry in 1978. In addition, many major carriers prefer to

Figure 6.1
Equipment Leasing Comparisons

Type of Equipment	Type of Lease	Lease Term (Years) Range	Weighted Average	Residual Value Assumptions Range	Weighted Average	Approximate Monthly	Monthly Payments* Annualized	Average Years to 100% Recovery
Aircraft								
New large commercial	Full payout	8-20	14.5	10-30%	21.5%	0.7908%	9.49%	10.54
Previously owned commercial	Operating	3-7	4	30-40%	35.0%	1.20%	14.40%	6.94
Computers								
Mainframe	Full payout	3-6	4.5	0-21%	7.3%	2-2.2%	26.4%	3.79
Peripheral	Operating	1-3	2	50-70%	60%	2.4-2.7%	31.2%	3.21
Industrial Equipment								
Material handling	Full payout	7-10	9	20-25%	21.0%	1.4-1.5%	18.0%	5.56
Manufacturing								
Numeric machine tools, etc.	Full payout	5-20	9.4	0-26%	7.8%	1.5-1.6%	17.4%	5.75
Railroad								
New	Full payout	6-21	15.5	0-25%	18.4%	1.2-1.3%	15.0%	6.67
Previously owned	Operating	3-5	3.5	50-75%	65.0%	1.6-1.7%	20.4%	4.90
Telecommunications								
Switching equipment		5-10	6.0	0-15%	15-20%	1.6-1.7	20.4%	4.90
Vehicles								
Tractors	Operating	5-11	5.5-8	20-50%	10.1%	1.5-1.8%	19.8%	5.05
Trailers	Operating	3-7	5	10-35%	24%	1.9-2.0%	23.4%	4.27
Cogeneration								
300kW	Full payout	5-7	6.5	10-25%	17.5%	1.5-2.1%	21.6%	4.63

* Not including residual vales

Source: American Association of Equipment Lessors; M.J. Held & Associates, Inc., various equipment leasing Partnership Sponsors.

Note: This document is for illustrative purposes only and should not be considered as absolute. Leasing rates, terms and residuals are ever changing items, each affecting the other.

acquire leased aircraft for a variety of reasons, to avoid borrowing or to manage short-term needs that better match short-haul, hub and spoke aircraft operations. Such operating leases are riskier but more profitable. On an annualized basis used aircraft lease income provides 14.40 percent of acquisition cost versus 9.49 percent for new aircraft. Residual values are also somewhat higher for used aircraft. This is because the acquisition cost for used aircraft is substantially less than for new aircraft but also because the erosion of residual value is greatest during the first half of the airplane's life.

In reviewing lease income rates for various equipment types listed in Figure 6.1, one can see that operating leases obtain the highest monthly rates. Obviously, the greater risk of these types of leases demand higher rentals. However, the risidual bet is also much more risky for these types of leases. If, for example, the bottom drops out of the market for a particular type of equipment—say for computer disk drives—then the leasing operator can be held holding the disk drive with no takers for release or renewal. Such a possibility is entirely possible in this illustration when you know that IBM dominates this mainframe peripheral market to such an extent that a simple new product introduction by the Armonk, NY-based computer company will utterly rearrange the market for computer disk drives.

Used Versus New Equipment

Used equipment provides opportunities for greater profits to the leasing partnership. For example, the used equipment can be leased under full-payout or operating leases to medium-size companies who need the equipment but are unable to buy the new equipment. Opportune buys of the used equipment are also possible as more of the leasing industry consolidates. What happens is that smaller leasing firms that are less able to compete for tax-oriented leases with the major lenders and lessors, are selling off their equipment portfolios to bargain-hunters among independent leasing operators, including some leasing partnerships. These *scavenger funds* aim to acquire used equipment at bargain-basement prices and turn around and lease them at prevailing lease rates.

Lease Structure Strategies

Another way to generate high income in leasing partnerships is to focus on the credit risk while minimizing the equipment risk.

For example, a full-payout lease can obtain substantially higher lease income if a leasing operator deals effectively with the riskier lessees. Lessees come in all sizes and shapes, but a skilled lessor can negotiate higher lease rates effectively with these middle-level credit risks. In these cases, the leasing operator minimizes the residual risk with a full-payout lease that is geared to recover the equipment cost in as little time as possible under a firm 'hell or high water' lease contract. All this colorful language indicates is that the lessor is assured of a firm leasing contract under full-payout terms.

One leasing partnership leases standard phone switching equipment to lesser credits under full-payout leases that average four to five years. However, because the lessor is dealing with lesser credit customers, he is able to charge rentals that permit a recovery period of 18 to 24 months, or less than half of the term of the lease. The residual value bet is effectively minimized, remarketing is of less concern, and the cash flow is entirely satisfactory—so long as the lessor has carefully picked his customers to avoid high default rates and/or has obtained upfront lease commitment fees or initial escrow deposits to help protect his credit risk.

Reinvestment Strategies

Income funds require substantial reinvestment of cash flow to expand and protect the partnership's equipment portfolio. This is often overlooked, but it is an important feature of the long-term success of a leasing income fund.

A leasing fund general partner cannot rest on his laurels. As described earlier, the business of equipment leasing is a lot like running a candy store—constant turnover of assets is necessary to keep the investment producing income over the long pull.

To successfully protect or expand the partnership's asset base, the leasing fund general partner will choose from among several options to continually build the productive capacity of the portfolio.

Occasionally some amount of debt leverage is called for, but not too much or fixed interest payments will reduce cash distributions to the limited partners and thwart the purpose of the income fund in the first place. There are all sorts of rules-of-thumb in determining how much debt is just enough in an income fund but most observers believe 20 to 50 percent is about the outer limit of fund indebtedness.

Another reinvestment strategy is to focus on only a limited type of equipment, new or used, that permit advantageous buys for fund investment. Volume buying can reduce acquisition costs for the partnership. One version of this is the use of vendor leasing programs by leasing partnership managers. In these cases, the partnership agrees to be the leasing subsidiary for the manufacturer or distributor. Usually the lessor is able to obtain purchase discounts from the vendor in return for providing the lease financing for the vendor's customers. In effect, the lessor is leveraging his equipment purchase dollars by developing an ongoing program with the vendor. The downside here is obvious: the leasing operator can become tied to the vendor and if the vendor catches a cold, the leasing operator can contract pneumonia. This occurred a few years ago when Phoenix Leasing, a mature operator of equipment leasing funds since the early 1970s, almost went under when one of its major vendor equipment partners—Storage Technology Corp. (STC)—filed for bankruptcy. Phoenix was suddenly left holding more than 50 percent of its partnership assets in STC equipment, whose value it was thought would plummet into the earth overnight. But Phoenix was able to hang on through a couple of years of skillful remarketing and lease management. So vendor lease programs also present risks to the fund equipment manager.

Another leasing partnership reinvestment strategy is to enter into joint ventures with other companies in the acquisition of equipment. Such joint ventures are typically undertaken with affiliates of the general partner or with other leasing partnerships managed by the general partner. Again, the aim is to leverage dollars of the partnership to obtain more equipment less expensively through volume buys. However, as pointed out earlier, such joint ventures carry the risk of conflicts of interest where the specific needs of the partnership may take second or third place.

What a financial advisor and investor should look for among leasing partnerships is a definite plan for reinvestment. The reinvestment plan should form an essential part of all financial projections. The strategies for reinvestment should be spelled out in advance. In addition to cash distribution targets, the financial investigator should ask for the reinvestment targets of the fund. How much of cash flow will be reinvested in additional partnership equipment? On what basis? How much in each year of the program? Used or new equipment? How much debt will be used? Will the portfolio be diversified to minimize the risk of equipment obsolescence? And most important, what sort of subordination will the general partner guarantee limited partners? For example, are the general partner's management fees substantially subordinated to the stated goals of protecting investor capital through reinvestment? These are all questions to ask the offering partnership sponsor.

There are always trade offs in determining how much cash flow in any business should be returned to investors and how much should be reinvested in the operation. There is a balance that must be achieved, but it is important to note that reinvestment on some definite basis is an essential part of the leasing income fund.

7
Leasing Growth Funds

The principal aim of equipment leasing growth funds is to generate long-term investor gains through appreciation of fund assets. To achieve this general aim, the growth fund typically sacrifices current cash distributions to build the investment portfolio while protecting investor capital contributions.

Growth funds adopt an investment plan that can take several forms. These include:

- The use of debt to leverage equipment acquisition and thus increase overall investor yields while—one hopes—still protecting investor capital

- A reinvestment strategy that maximizes long-term asset growth over current cash distribution

- An operating strategy that seeks out longer-term full payout leases where the investor's comfort level is more important than high income but riskier lease rates. The bet on managing operating leases or wagering on anticipated residual values is minimized. Credit risk is minimized in favor of long-term security. With this operating strategy, low-obsolescence equipment—for example, railcars or containers—are managed under full-payout leases to only the most creditworthy lessees. Proceeds are then substantially reinvested to expand the asset base rather than distributing more of the operating income back to investors on a current basis.

There are problems with leasing growth funds which have diminished their interest in the limited partnership marketplace. The major problem with them is that with recent tax reform, investors are looking for current income over long-term appreciation. In effect, the investor is saying: "Give me my cash now. There is no tax advantage to long-term capital gains versus current income. I'd rather have the cash today and reinvest it myself rather than depend on you to reinvest it for me over the next 10 to 15 years."

The Use of Debt

The basic method of building long-term investor growth in leasing funds is through the use of debt to leverage investment in the equipment. The idea is that long-term yields are better if each investor dollar can be leveraged to add more income-producing assets. But how much debt is enough? This is the problem with leveraged leasing programs.

For example, let's compare a leasing fund with zero debt versus one that used 50 percent leverage. Let's assume we have equal types of programs, in this illustration a fund that invests in computer peripheral equipment, yielding about the same annual lease income. Further, let's assume that both funds operate very similarly; over a five-year period both distribute the same percentage of cash flow to investors and obtain roughly the same release and residual values on the equipment.

Here's how the comparison might look like:

Figure 7.1
Leasing Leverage

	#1 Fund Zero Debt	#2 Fund 50% Debt
Initial Stage		
Investment	$10,000	$10,000
Equipment purchase	8,500	16,000*

(continued)

First Operating Stage (Years 1-3)

Revenues (30 percent/yr)	7,650	14,400
Debt cost	0	8,640**
Overhead (10 percent revenue)	765	1,400
Cash distributed (15 percent of investment)	1,500	1,500
Amount reinvested	5,385	2,860

* 15 percent deducted for management fees in #1 Fund. Less 20 percent for leveraged fund because of extra equipment.

** With prevailing interest rates at about 10 percent, 60 percent of gross revenues will amortize the debt in three years.

Second Operating Stage (Years 4 & 5)

New equipment bought	5,385	2,860
New equipment revenue (30 percent per year)	3,231	1,716
Release revenue (24 percent per year)	4,080	7,680
Overhead (10 percent revenues)	723	939
Net revenue, 2nd stage	6,588	8,457
15 percent cash distributed	1,500	1,500
Cash available	4,088	6,957

If we stopped here, you can see how the leveraged leasing fund would continue to generate greater revenue than the unleveraged fund because it will have more equipment earning income on subsequent release of the equipment. According to this scenario, once the original debt is paid off, the leveraged fund will generate greater returns as the program matures. The longer the fund's life, the better the returns. Right? Not necessarily.

What is missing in this equation is one very important ingredient—the cost of money, to the investor and to the partnership. If, for example, loan interest rates should rise, the entire equation might change. Most equipment financing loans would be pegged at floating prime rates which could accelerate very quickly and dramatically increase the cost of money. That could prove disastrous to the partnership. A prime rate increase of, say, 2 percent, from 10 to 12 percent could happen in a few weeks. That would be a 20 percent increase in debt payments which would easily wipe out cash flow projections for Fund # 2 in the previous illustration.

Some argue that leasing investments are a good inflation hedge, and this is true up to a point. But lease rates cannot easily be raised automatically with an increase in the lessor's cost of money. And besides, the loan covenants imposed by the lender to the partnership may mandate working capital reserves or require cross-collateralization of other fund assets to the extent that the risks to the entire partnership would be magnified.

Reinvestment Alternatives

A more compelling reason for not having too much debt or any debt at all is that debt will reduce cash distributions during the early operating years of the program, in which case, the investor has less of an opportunity to reinvest his own cash distribution in other alternative investments. This is especially true for equipment leasing investments which must compete in the first place among all sorts of alternative investments in the financial services marketplace.

For example, an equipment leasing income fund must produce higher cash returns than money markets, CDs and top rated corporate bonds. Higher cash returns from leasing partnerships are necessary to offset the yields, liquidity and perceived safety of these other investments to attract the investor. If cash yields fall to 5 percent a year (versus 12 to 15 percent promised) on a leasing fund and money markets deliver 7 percent, the investor is losing money. The investor would prefer to have that cash for reinvestment rather than have the leasing partnership reinvest it for him if the eventual result is simply a lower overall investor internal rate of return.

Comfort Level Versus Growth

Some funds that have promoted the idea of growth have usually sought to deal with the insecurities of the investor more than pursue a long-term program of asset appreciation. Some examples include both the leasing operation structure or through a device of investing fund proceeds in zero coupon bonds.

In order to overcome investor fears about the depleting value of equipment, some funds have promoted the use of zero coupon bonds to build investor capital in parallel with the partnership's leasing activities. It works like this: the fund promises to return the investor's capital at the end of the program's life by taking a portion of the cash operating proceeds and investing it in a side zero coupon investment. The aim is simple enough but the results for the investor are no better, and perhaps worse than what the investor can do for himself or herself.

A like-minded approach by some leasing partnerships described as growth funds is to invest in equipment leased to blue chip companies under full-payout leases than ensure the recovery of the partnership's investment. Such investments tend to give the appearance of investor safety, but in reality suffer in comparison with alternative investments because investor internal rates of return are insufficient. The problems are several. First, leasing partnerships must generate sufficient cash flow to offset high initial frontloads in limited partnership syndication. Second, partnerships are at a disadvantage in competing for full-payout leases among blue-chip lessees. These are essentially finance-oriented leases where major lenders have a keen advantage in access to capital and where the price bidding for the lease busines drives lease income rates low. In effect, a partnership that structures a growth fund with a conservative leasing structure does not create much growth for the investor and only promotes security for the investor.

Some of this reasoning helps explain why so-called growth funds are not especially attractive. But it all depends on the type of investor. The object of good financial planning is to match up investment risks and rewards with the right type of investor. The balancing of risks and rewards is an ongoing process in the financial services industry. In some cases a diversified equipment leasing strategy can provide the right mix of risks and rewards for an investor. In chapter 14, for instance, we'll discuss a growing trend among some financial advisors to recommend a portfolio mix of equipment leasing partnerships that blend risks and rewards in a single leasing investment strategy.

In subsequent chapters of this book, we'll explore more deeply the types of equipment that are included in public leasing partnerships. The equipment itself and the structure of the leasing strategy can provide both a means for current income and long-term growth of the partner's assets under management.

8

Computer Funds

Starting with the introduction of equipment leasing partnerships in the early 1970s, computer funds have been among the most popular with investors. The reason is fairly straightforward: the computer industry is among the fastest growing in the United States. Some enthusiasts go so far as to say that the "business of business is data." There is more than a grain of truth to this claim. One industry research source predicted that more than $200 billion of new computer equipment would be acquired in the U.S. between 1988-92. These kind of numbers also benefit leasing activities.

Figure 8.1 demonstrates that computer leasing is also the leader among all equipment leasing categories. The rate of growth of new computer leasing business continues to outstrip other types of equipment leasing. The computer industry is also a widespread, diverse, and fast-changing business that is well suited to leasing in general and to leasing partnerships in particular.

Nearly two of every three new equipment leasing funds offered in the past several years has promised to invest principally in computers and computer-related equipment. Why? The answer is that aside from computer industry growth, computer leasing economics fit the niche of leasing partnerships extremely well. Additionally, for many investors, unfortunately, computers are also sexy. An investment is computer leasing may give the investor the feeling that he or she is "with it."

Of more consequence to leasing fund economics is that computers provide a means to generate high current cash flow to provide the yields investors must have to take a plunge into the world of leasing partnerships.

Figure 8.1
Total Annual Leasing Volume
(% of new leasing business by operation)

Operation	1985	1986
Computers	20.7	26
Other	17.9	12.5
Aircraft	13.7	10.4
Communications	9.6	11.8
Office Machines	8.5	8.8
Trucks & Trailers	7.5	6.9
Manufacturing	5.2	5
Industrial	4.9	6.2
Project	3.5	4.2
Railroad	2.8	1.7
Medical	2.7	2.8
Construction	2.5	2.4
Agriculture	0.5	1.7

■ 1985
▨ 1986

Leasing Computers

Computer leasing funds have tended to invest primarily in computer peripheral equipment—tape and disk drives, tape controllers, printers, card readers, and other devices. Computer terminal systems are another favorite fund investment. These types of computer equipment have tended to hold their future value more than mainframe computers in recent years, mainly because microprocessor technology has been moving rapidly and expanding central processing unit power at a dramatic rate.

To a lesser extent, the computer leasing funds also invest in mainframe computer systems for small and medium-size businesses. Office and telecommunications equipment and research and measuring equipment are also acquired by leasing funds under the general heading of computers.

Any mention of computers casts the dominant shadow of IBM on all marketing activities. Any change in IBM marketing or pricing activities or new introductions can dramatically disrupt the computer marketplace overnight. Because the pace of change is so rapid in the computer equipment business, the use of operating leases has become a very important means of financing sale and use of the equipment. The fear of technological and market changes far outweighs the risk of physical obsolescence and encourages the choice of leasing by many equipment users. New advances in computing technology, new software introductions, and pricing changes exert a powerful influence on computer equipment economics, primarily on residual values.

Equipment Diversification

Financial advisors should look for equipment diversification in computer funds. Being tied to any one vendor or any one type of equipment makes the investment a riskier venture. Some leasing funds prefer to invest almost exclusively in IBM equipment but this is not always that wise. First, it costs more to acquire IBM equipment, but also IBM can change all the rules with a new product introduction. One saving ingredient for most IBM remarketers is that IBM continues to maintain a long-standing policy of customer service on used IBM equipment which tends to support the aftermarket for IBM equipment.

Very often, a leasing fund sponsor will want to obtain lower cost equipment than IBM sells. This doesn't necessarily mean inferior equipment, as many smaller computer makers have demonstrated. In some specialized computer markets—in engineering and for midrange computer users, computer makers like Digital Equipment Corp., Hewlett-Packard, Compaq, Apple Computer, and others have demonstrated a strength equal or better than IBM.

A good guideline that a leasing manager might use is to avoid more than 50 percent fund investment in any one computer vendor, even IBM, although it depends on what equipment diversification is desired. As for equipment selected for fund portfolios, a mix of computer equipment and even other types of equipment that are not tied to computer industry vagaries (transportation, industrial, medical, and others) might be a good choice to diversify some of the risks of obsolescence inherent in the computer industry.

Computer Residuals

Figure 8.2 shows just how quickly residual values erode for basic computer peripheral equipment. New IBM small system mainframes and disks have almost a zero effective value in just five years. But remember, these are only estimates. It could be worse.

It has happened more than once in the past couple of years that a product introduction from IBM has completely wiped out the residual values of competing products held for investment by equipment leasing funds. One sad case featured a leasing sponsor who completely walked away from the no name equipment managed by the fund after IBM changed its marketing policies on disk drives.

If computers are so risky, why do leasing funds invest in them? That answer is equally simple: operating lease rates on computer equipment are extraordinarily high. Figure 8.3 shows typical net monthly lease rates for new IBM equipment on one, two, and three-year operating leases. For example, a two-year lease on an IBM 3090 mainframe generates a 2.65 percent monthly lease rate. This means that in 24 months the lessor will recover 63.6 percent of the original retail cost of the equipment. At that point, the expected residual value of the IBM 3090 will be between 36 and 42 percent. But let's say the lessor releases that equipment for two years to another client at 2.65 percent, he will recover another 63.6 percent of the original equipment cost, or 127.2 percent for the four-year period.

Figure 8.2
Computer Residual Assumptions

New IBM Equipment	Equipment No.	Jan. 88 0 years	Jan. 89 1 year	Jan. 90 2 years	Jan. 91 3 years	Jan. 92 4 years	Jan. 93 5 years
Mainframe	3090-600E	New	60-66%	36-42%	21-22%	9-11%	0-6%
Printer (laser)	3800-006	New	98%	93%	73%	64%	48%
Disk	9335-A01	New	85-88%	70-71%	51-52%	30-38%	0-18%
Terminal	3174-1R	New	68-74%	55-57%	35-45%	22-36%	10-24%

Source: International Data Corporation
Daley Marketing Corporation

Figure 8.3
Monthly Lease Rate Scenario
Various Types of Computer Equipment at Retail Original Cost

New IBM Equipment	Equipment No.	1 Year	2 Years	3 Years
Mainframe	3090-600E	3.18%	2.65%	2.30%
Printer (laser)	3800-006	1.74%	1.59%	1.22%
Disk Storage	9335-A01	2.03%	1.74%	1.69%
Terminal	3174-1R	1.96%	1.94%	1.94%

Source: International Data Corporation. Daley Marketing Corporation.

Prepared by: M.J. Held & Associates, Inc.

The residual value at this point is estimated to be between 9 and 11 percent. If the lessor just sells the equipment, he will recover a total of about 137 percent of the original retail investment in four years, enough to cover lease operating costs and provide a modest profit.

The economics can grow even better for the lessor by acquiring the equipment at wholesale prices but especially by keeping the equipment on renewal beyond the second lease. As a practical matter, computer lessors do best when the equipment is successfully remarketed beyond the second lease. The key is to keep the equipment on lease beyond the recovery period. As we've shown before in chapter 3, residual value projections are decisive in the investment analysis of computer leasing. No one has a crystal ball on future values of computer equipment, and this makes the investment decision much more problematical for the prospective limited partner.

Judging Computer Residuals

To some the art of calculating computer residuals is very difficult. To others, the process may even be deceitful. And to the gullible, the rosier the projection the better. Between these approaches, a financial advisor should be able to effectively question the sponsor of a leasing fund on residual and lease rate assumptions.

Somewhere deep in the spreadsheets of a leasing fund sponsor's financial projections for broker/dealers and financial advisors is an effective residual value scenario. It is a number. First, one must find out the number or the range of residual value assumptions explicit in the financial projection. This is not always easy to extract but good due diligence requires this information. OK. Now you have a residual value assumption. What do you do with it? Test it.

How was the residual assumption arrived at? You already know the answer—it is the sponsor's best guess, yes *guess*—but find out why this particular assumption was made. How does the residual assumption for this particular equipment compare with computer residual research firms' projections? The sponsor should be a subscriber to some of these computer information services, the most notable being International Data Corporation (IDC), the Gartner Group, Arthur D. Little, Marshall & Stevens, Computer Economics, or American Appraisals.

Computer residual estimates provide a range of outcomes over a number of future years. Best case, worst case, and likely case scenarios will provide a range of outcomes on the fund's financial projections or estimates. (By the way, do not expect any of this information in the sponsor's prospectus. The Securities and Exchange Commission which registers all publicly offered limited partnerships discourages the use of projections in the investor offering statement. Unfortunately, some sponsors may take this to mean they can hide behind the boilerplate of the prospectus and avoid mention of any residual assumption.)

The financial advisor or planner will see two sorts of guesses about residual value assumptions in the financial projections. The first is the residual value itself and the second is the lease rate assumption, which is highly dependent on residual predictions. The next step is to compare these residual assumptions or scenarios against the actual history of the leasing fund general partner's actual performance in prior funds. Some of this lease rate and residual value history is included in the prospectus but better that the sponsor provide a weighted average of historical residual values and lease rates for particular types of equipment from prior operating experience. How do the residual projections compare to prior sponsor performance? Too high? Then reduce them to obtain a more realistic gauge of future residuals and lease rates.

Conservative residual assumptions should always be used in developing financial projections. Assume the worst case.

Remarketing Expertise

It should be obvious that computer leasing is a fast- paced, ever-changing business that requires hands-on management. Computer leasing partnerships, in particular, tend to deal mostly with lower-ticket computer equipment. This means many, many leases, lessees, and pieces of equipment. This back room activity requires substantial general partner overhead in people and systems to control the whole process. This costs money. Beware the fund sponsor that tries to gloss over this investment in overhead. After all, you as the investor are paying the general partner very substantial operating and management fees for this necessary investment in people and systems.

The remarketing of computer equipment—renewing the lease, releasing to another lessee or selling the equipment— is an extensive process that requires highly skilled and experienced sponsor personnel. An important consideration for the financial advisor is to determine how well the general partner has financed his operation

The fear among many knowledgeable sources in the leasing business is that more than one computer leasing fund sponsor has sold the sizzle of the partnership without committing to the operation of the leasing management side. This is a real concern and financial advisors should be cautious and should demand a real performance history from fund sponsors.

Cash distributions can be deceptive, too. A sponsor may only be returning more capital than profits during the early years of the computer fund's life. Real profits do not start showing up until the third operating lease, often not until the program has gone four to five years. So avoid computer leasing program sponsors that have not demonstrated a record over at least this period—either as a fund sponsor or as a *bona fide* leasing operator. If the sponsor's only evidence of future residual value is to be found in the screen of a crystal ball, then it might be wise to consider another fund.

9

Aircraft Funds

Investors put $500 million into aircraft leasing limited partnerships in 1987—almost 40 percent of all dollars invested in leasing funds that year. For many of these investors the lure could be explained by sponsor claims that these funds that acquire and lease commercial jet aircraft are an ideal bet: good cash yields, low risk, and some tax benefits. For others owning a piece of an airplane seems to have special significance. But the potential investor in these aircraft leasing funds should look carefully before he or she gets on board. Airplanes are not about to go out of fashion, but the economics of the commercial airline business is a very tricky business.

In this chapter, we want to explore the dynamics of the commercial airline business, because the aircraft leasing marketplace may be one of the most complex among all those offered in the leasing funds business.

Airline Economics

Let's start off with the U.S. airline industry which has gone through many changes since the industry was deregulated in 1978. In ten short years, the industry has turned around. But aside from the bankruptcies, mergers, and consolidations, the air controller strike in the early 1980s, and the emergence of new startup carriers, the U.S. air carrier industry has been fundamentally changed in its economics.

Prior to deregulation, major carriers held oligarchic control of routes and fares. Cost was not much of an issue because you could simply petition the Civil Aeronautics Board (CAB) for a rate hike.

Airline management prior to deregulation were on a high-flying merry-go-round. Heavy debt-to-equity was commonplace. Why not? The banks looked at the airlines as cash cows. So long as the carriers could raise fares to pay off airplane debt and interest, who cared? But, as we all know, deregulation changed everything.

For an industry that had been run from a country club for decades, airline managers suddenly had to compete for travelers among a lot of new entrants and mature carriers that moved into their traditional routes. The crunch hit almost immediately. The strong, well-financed carriers, such as Delta and American Airlines, have been able to adapt to the new, competitive marketplace. Others, such as Braniff and Eastern, were hit hard. New carriers came and went. Some stooped to conquer, like aggressively managed Continental.

In all this change over the past decade, the traditional financing of commercial aircraft was also changed. No longer was money easily available. The operation of the air transport system moved to a hub-and-spoke system where efficiencies of airplane and route management were obtained but which now required new fleets of short-haul, efficient airplanes such as enhanced 737s and DC9s to compete more effectively. Older Boeing 727 aircraft had to be replaced with new Boeing jets like the 757 or 767 and Airbus A300s and A310s. Startups sought used aircraft to enter the skies that had been opened to them. New means of financing acquisition of these aircraft—new and used—had to be found, and leasing was a natural, particularly because aircraft leased under operating leases provided operational flexibility in a swiftly changing marketplace. Some industry experts say that 30 percent of the 7,000 commercial jet aircraft flying today in North America is leased.

Aircraft Leasing Funds

Polaris Aircraft (now controlled by General Electric Credit Corporation) was one of the first in the early 1980s to see the value of using limited partnerships to raise equity to acquire commercial aircraft for its existing aviation leasing business. Others have joined the field so that today a number of partnership sponsors are actively engaged in aircraft leasing funds.

For the most part, these aircraft leasing syndicators focus on a particular airline financing niche—principally used jet aircraft that is suited to the short-haul, hub-and spoke-system of U.S. air transport.

The reason for this is that such aircraft can be obtained relatively cheaply versus the cost of new jet airplanes. For example, a 15-year-old DC-9-30 which is still in good condition will cost about $3 to 4 million versus a new version MD80 that will run about $22 million.

Of importance to the leasing of these used airplanes is that operating lease rates can be very attractive, particularly on the expectation that used jet aircraft have held their value pretty well in the past 5 to 10 years. Some estimates predict that 20 percent of all commercial aircraft will be financed under operating leases by 1990. This is an enormous potential market for independent lessors, including leasing fund syndicators.

Evaluating Risks

Despite the appeal of aircraft leasing and aircraft leasing partnerships, these funds are highly complex in terms of their economics and technical analysis. To properly evaluate these funds requires an understanding of how the business works in a highly charged economic environment. It is also a very cyclical business that is highly dependent on the U.S. general economy.

As in all operating leases, the economics is weighted toward the buying and remarketing of the equipment under lease management. As competition for this airline lease business stiffens, the pressure on obtaining profitable leases and successfully remarketing the airplane equipment becomes one where technical expertise is crucial. Let's take one illustration that involves aircraft noise regulations.

The key issue again is residual value of the used aircraft which is largely determined by the anticipated market value of the airplane, not just its physical condition. For example, tougher noise regulations are likely to have a substantial impact on used aircraft equipment residuals because most of the 7,000 commercial jets flying in 1988 do not meet new Federal Aviation Administration (FAA) noise reduction standards. The new standards are expected to cause many of these aircraft to be phased out starting in the middle 1990s. Unless these aircraft are not brought up to meet federal regulations with hush kits and noise reduction devices (which can run into the millions of dollars), then their future value will drop significantly, well below residual predictions of just a couple of years ago.

Some airline experts see a soft market for used aircraft until 1993. While passenger air traffic continues to grow about 5 to 6 percent a year in the U.S., airlines have been adding new available seats at the rate of 12 to 17 percent in recent years, up until 1988. If the general economy turns down, the growth in passenger traffic could drop down to 1 to 2 percent or no growth at all, forcing many carriers to sell off large numbers of their airplane fleet. Some of this has occurred with Eastern Airlines after it was acquired by Continental Airlines. With these kinds of economic disruptions, used aircraft can appear in large numbers at any given time, which would drive down values substantially.

Figure 9.1 shows the life cycle of used short-and-medium range commercial jet aircraft. These 727, DC9, and 737 aircraft have a physical life span of roughly 30 years in service. For the first 20 years of their life, these aircraft hold up in service very well—almost 90 percent are still flying, but then the life of these planes drop precipitously. In five more years, to illustrate, the percentage of these aircraft surviving will drop from close to 90 percent in service to less than 20 percent. But this is only the physical life of these airplanes. The economic degradation of their value on the used aircraft marketplace is subject to any number of economic uncertainties.

The uncertainty of any equipment residual value is a sure thing, but some aircraft leasing fund sponsors have been very optimistic about future values of these airplanes. For example, one sponsor included a residual assumption of 100 percent for a 15-year-old Boeing 727 at the end of the next 12 years after the plane was acquired by the partnership. At 27 years old, this aircraft would be near the end of its physical life and would in almost any likely scenario be worth little more than its scrap metal value.

In making such optimistic residual value forecasts on used airplanes, leasing syndicators are banking very heavily on inflation. It is a mistake to project residuals on such high-blown inflation estimates. It may happen but such an inflation factor does not really deal with the underlying economics of the used aircraft business.

Checking Out Sponsor Claims

Some ways to offset an overly optimistic assumption from creeping into aircraft leasing investor projections is to review the history of the general partner and sponsor. Are projected aircraft lease rates in line with the history of the aircraft lease operator? How *conservative* are the assumptions on residuals? Are these residuals backed up by

**Figure 9.1
Survivor Curve
Short and Medium-Range Jet Transports**

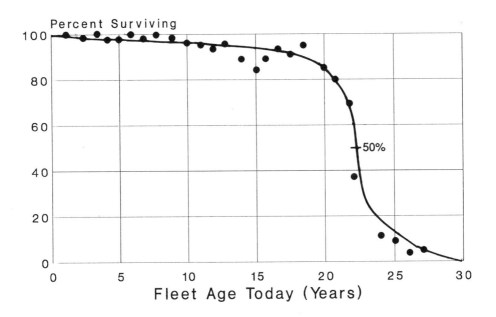

general partner experience and independent appraisals of the aircraft under consideration?

The financial advisor also needs to wonder which airline will acquire the used aircraft from the partnership. If at all possible, the advisor and investor should want good credit carriers as customers. There have been one too many merger or bankruptcies to be free-wheeling about potential airline lessees.

Does the general partner require special lease covenants that protect the partnership in the case of bankruptcy or default on the lease? Aircraft leases can be so structured as to protect the lessor against almost any contingency. Such covenants permit the immediate recovery of the equipment in case of default, regardless of other creditor claims on the carrier.

Does the aircraft fund sponsor provide a clear identity of interest with the investor? For example, are acquisition and operating fees reasonable? In many cases general partner fee percentages should be lower in an aircraft leasing fund because the nature of the lease acquisition and transactions does not involve as significant an overhead to maintain and manage the leases as does another equipment fund with many more pieces of equipment, leases, and lessees. Besides, the dollar value of aircraft leasing funds are traditionally much higher at full subscription than for other types of equipment funds. For example, the typical aircraft leasing fund aims for a total investment subscription of about $100 million per fund, as compared to a publicly offered computer leasing fund that can range from $5 million to $50 million. The sponsor should be willing to take lower acquisition, operating, and liquidation percentage fees because his effort and costs do not easily justify the high fee percentages.

Additionally, the aircraft sponsor should be willing to subordinate more of the management fee to later stages of the program in favor of ongoing investor returns or reinvestment. This identity with investor interests should be a point of distinction in evaluating any equipment leasing sponsor, but it helps if an investor or financial advisor understand more clearly just how much confidence the sponsor has in his own projections, most of which is dependent on the liquidation stage of the program.

It is also a good idea that the leasing management of the fund require so-called triple net leases which mean that the carrier leasing the equipment is responsible for all maintenance, insurance, and taxes. Such costs are a significant cost in the operation of FAA-registered commercial aircraft.

Aircraft leasing funds can be a successful investment for the limited partners. Our caveats stress two important criteria for evaluation. First, the airline industry is a gamble. It is a fast-changing business. As airline stocks tend to be speculative, so, too, is the airline industry. Know what you're getting into. Second, a high degree of aviation technical expertise along with leasing and financial know-how is required of any aircraft leasing general partner. Look for this fund management track record.

One way of avoiding the risks inherent in investing in a single type of equipment—such as used commercial jet aircraft or computers—is to invest in a leasing fund that seeks to diversify its equipment risks or to seek out equipment, such as cargo containers, which minimize the residual risk.

10

Diversified Transportation Funds

So far we have described two types of high-tech equipment—computers and aircraft—which are popular equipment investments for leasing limited partnerships. But low-tech equipment can be profitable, too. The best examples of low-tech equipment investment by leasing funds are illustrated by what are called *diversified transportation equipment funds.*

Transportation equipment is the single largest equipment category for leasing. Almost $32 billion of transportation equipment was leased in the U.S. in 1986. While much of this leasing activity financed large capital investments, such as ships, jet airplanes, railroads, and, of course, the automobile, a significant amount of leasing activity also went into low tech transportation equipment such intermodal containers, rail freight cars, truck tractors, and trailers.

Low-Tech Economics

Many investors might wonder just how low-tech equipment could be very profitable, particularly for an equipment leasing fund, which requires high cash current yields to attract investors. The success of these funds lies not so much in the admittedly mundane equipment but in how this equipment, is managed.

Typically, lease operators of transportation equipment rely more on the aggressive management of equipment and credit risks rather than on the residual value of the equipment. The weight of the leasing activity is shifted because the residual risk is much more predictable for most types of diversified equipment. Let's take marine containers as a prime example.

Container Leasing

Containers are as low-tech as you get. For example, trailers hitched to the back of a tractor truck are composed of just three elements: aluminum, rubber, and labor. Sturdily constructed to standard specifications, there's no great fear that they will go out of fashion very soon or that any technological breakthrough is going to disrupt the market.

Intermodal containers started to come into wider use in the early 1970s. The idea among shippers and container makers was to arrive at standard-size container units that would provide for greater convenience and flexibility and reduce handling costs. Today marine containers come in two basic flavors: 20- and 40-foot dry containers. There are some specialized containers such as refrigerated units or tank cars that carry liquids and a couple of other types such as chassis containers for loading on truck tractors or even double-stack rail car containers, but that's about all the variety the shipping industry needs.

There are about 5 million TEUs of containers in use today in the world. (A TEU = twenty-foot equivalent unit and is the standard measure of container capacity used by the shipping industry.) Of this world marine container fleet, one half is owned and leased by independent leasing firms while the other half is owned by the shippers. The number and percentage of containers that are leased has been growing steadily over the years (see Figure 10.1).

The leased container business has developed because the shipping and rail industry has sought to reduce its own capital investments, which are substantial, and to gain greater flexibility in the world shipping business.

The life of these containers extends to about 20 years or more. Residual values are very predictable. Normally, these containers retain about 60 percent of their original cost after about 12 to 15 years. Even then there is a considerable secondary use for the containers for fixed storage, and, sadly, for use in the Third World as basic habitat for homeless and poor people.

Like a Rental Business

Containers are usually leased for short periods of time under master lease programs. In effect, industry experts say, container leasing is like renting a car. Short-term rental rates reflect the convenience and

Figure 10.1
Leasing Company Share of Total Container Fleet

Millions TEU's

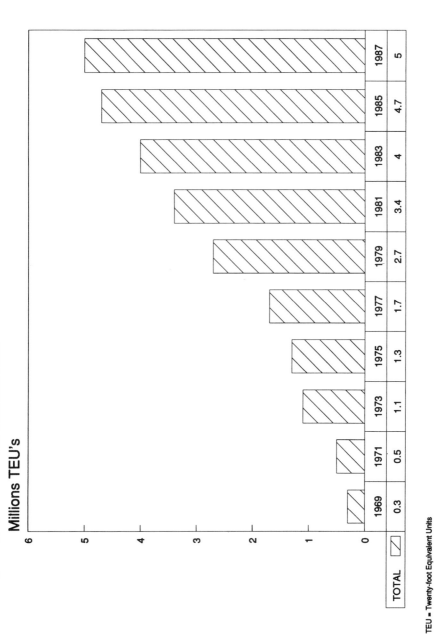

TOTAL	1969	1971	1973	1975	1977	1979	1981	1983	1985	1987
	0.3	0.5	1.1	1.3	1.7	2.7	3.4	4	4.7	5

TEU = Twenty-foot Equivalent Units

Source: Containerisation International Yearbook 1987.

flexibility of using cars only when you have a need. It is a service business that charges for that service. For a shipper really asks: what do I do with the container once I deliver the product? Ownership is not the decisive issue for the carriers.

Container Industry Economics

Leased container annual revenues in the world was about $5 billion in 1987. And this is a world market, subject to supply and demand pressures from a group of international players. Like a car rental company, container leasing companies are able to obtain high short-term rentals (in relation to the equipment investment cost), because they provide an efficient and flexible market for shippers. Container rental customers pay more for the flexibility, because it helps them weather trade volume fluctuations more efficiently. A shipper will pay more for destination charges on equipment that is dropped off in one port because it allows the shipper to avoid worry about finding more cargo on the return trip. Under terms of container master leases of one to two years in duration, shippers negotiate lease rates and terms, while allowing schedules, destinations, and quantities to be ordered as needed in short-term rentals.

You can begin to see that the key to successful container leasing is aggressive and experienced management. The ability to keep containers on lease, maintain high lease rates and acquire equipment efficiently are the hallmarks of an effective container lessor. It is a specialized leasing business. While more than 95 companies compete in this world container leasing marketplace, only two dozen firms control 90 to 95 percent of the world container leasing volume. But it is a highly competitive business that is subject to world trade economics, foreign currency fluctuations and container supply inconsistencies that may develop quickly—such as container overproduction from dominant suppliers in nations like Korea, Japan, and Poland.

Evaluating Transportation Equipment Funds

Transportation equipment leasing funds can adopt different strategies to produce high-cash investor distributions. In some cases, as we've mentioned for container leasing, aggressive management of short-term leases with major shippers is the key. In some cases, the reliance on used equipment and an aggressive reinvestment strategy can boost investor yields over the long-term. In other cases, the leasing strategy may also include higher lease rates by dealing more effectively with lesser credit risks. Another strategy may be to use full payout leases to major corporations with blue-chip credit ratings, because residual values are so predictable and lend greater support for preservation of partnership capital.

The financial advisor should be looking for deep experience in the management of the equipment from the general partner. In some cases, the public partnership offering may be made by one co-general partner who handles the financial and marketing side, with another co-general partner which manages and remarkets the equipment. This is sometimes preferable to a sponsor trying to do both the financial side and equipment management, when his basic expertise is in partnership syndication only. It is important that the general partner have special expertise in the specific equipment under management.

Another factor to consider is the mix of equipment acquired for the partnership. Equipment diversification can reduce risks to the partnership. A variety of equipment investment limits the reliance on any one or two types of equipment whose market value loss could hurt performance of the entire fund. Even in container leasing, a mix of specialized and standard containers should be evaluated for optimizing risk and rewards. For example, used and specialty containers will produce much higher profits per investment dollar than new standard dry containers. The question for the lease operator is: how much of a good thing is enough? A knowledgeable lessor will have already planned the mix of equipment types, but will have contingency reinvestment plans in case of market changes for the equipment. Ask to see these analyses and have the sponsor justify the investment choices in terms of investor yields.

While investors can obtain high current cash distributions from diversified transportation funds, they also provide a measure of investor security because of the low obsolescence of the equipment. It is easier to argue that these funds provide greater capital protection than more speculative investments in computer equipment, for example.

In our next chapter, we'll probe other types of diversified equipment leasing funds, ones that invest primarily in industrial and medical equipment.

11
Industrial and Medical Equipment Funds

The great majority of leasing public partnerships focus on the management of operating leases to generate high cash on-cash yields for investors. However, the same goal of high current income can be achieved through the effective management of standardized equipment such as industrial and medical equipment under conservative full-payout leases.

Relatively small-ticket equipment such as X-ray machines or material-handling equipment are still big business. Some equipment leasing funds take advantage of this fact of business and structure leasing funds that profitably use the primary variables of equipment leasing risk. These primary risks can be adjusted to suit a high-income leasing strategy even if the equipment is fairly standard. Aggressive equipment acquisition is the key to the success of this kind of equipment leasing fund.

Types of Equipment

Medical equipment is a rapidly growing market for leasing. Part of the reason is the unabated growth of the health care industry, which is the largest industry in the U.S. By 1990, according to the American Medical Association, U.S. health care costs will reach about $750 billion—almost 12 percent of gross national product. This is a staggering figure when you think about it, but it also demonstrates the growing use of medical equipment for testing and health management.

Public legislation involving catastrophic aid, Medicare, and

Medicaid as well as the health crisis posed by AIDS (Acquired Immune Deficiency Syndrome) continues to drive up the demand for medical technology used in diagnostic, surgical, patient-care, and health care management services. Some of this medical equipment is new but becoming more commonplace. Recent advances include computed tomography (CT) systems, magnetic imaging resonance (MRI) systems, sonography (ultrasound devices), and many others. The increase of litigation over medical negligence or malpractice has also spurred greater use of testing procedures. These trends have combined to further raise use of medical equipment, not just for more exotic systems but for standard medical equipment such as X-ray equipment, patient monitoring instruments, and lab testing devices.

In industrial and manufacturing settings, a large market exists for relatively standard types of production and material handling equipment. We're talking about relatively low-obsolescence equipment such as simple production conveyor systems, lift trucks, machine tool, and testing equipment, to name just a few.

Investment Strategy

Funds which invest in these standard types of industrial and medical and even low-tech transportation equipment (tractor/trailers, for example) aim to reduce equipment risk and boost limited partner investment protection by selecting standard equipment for lease under full payout leases. But they also seek to generate high cash yields by aggressively managing the credit risk for higher lease income rates. They also adopt a variety of equipment acquisition tactics to wring greater profits from the leasing operation. Let's review how these mid-level leasing funds manage the risks of equipment, credit, and equipment acquisition.

Equipment Risk

By choosing standard equipment with broad applications in many types of industries with numerous potential lessees, the general partner reduces the residual and remarketing risk of the equipment. With more predictable future values and a wide selection of possible lessees for the equipment, the leasing fund manager will find more takers for full-payout leases that will recover the original cost of the equipment. The residual bet is minimized. But can the lease operator get the kinds of lease rentals necessary to meet the investor test for an equipment leasing partnership? The answer is yes because credit risk and operating strategy can focus on those market niches were higher cash flow is possible.

Credit Risk

Lease operators of diversified equipment fund portfolios often look for middle-level credit risks where they can get higher rentals for even full payout leases. In effect, the independent lessor can compete more effectively against institutional lenders for medium-size credits who seek smaller-ticket equipment, such as is represented by an X-ray machine for a health clinic or lift trucks for a small manufacturer or industrial distributor.

Of course, this credit strategy requires that the leasing fund manager have the experience and management to deal effectively with less-than-the-best credits and numerous leases and pieces of equipment. The risk of lessee default is always present, but effective management of the credit risk is what makes leasing work in the first place. If a lessor has been in business for many years, the assumption is that this lessor can manage that credit risk because he knows what types of customers he needs to make it work. It's important that financial advisors look very carefully at the fund operator's lease default rate and compare it to industry norms for the equipment under management.

Equipment Acquisition Strategies

The real secret to managing primarily full-payout leasing funds involves the successful use of a number of tactics to increase the spread between equipment acquisition cost and lease rates. Here are some of the tactics used:

Lease Pool Acquisition.   Tax reform, has reduced the emphasis on tax-oriented leasing. In many cases, small independent leasing operators are getting out of the business. One way of getting out is to sell their equipment lease pools—at a heavy discount—to other lessors looking for bargains. What happens is that a larger lessor, such as a leasing fund operator, will acquire this small lessor's inventory of equipment and leases. Sometimes an institutional lender will also sell its lease pools, because it prefers not to be involved in the management of the leases. Thus, the new owner will often obtain the lease pool at a substantial discount in return for future lease income. These bargains are always available, but it takes a shrewd operator to make it work. The process involves the same principle as buying used equipment. If you know the equipment and the credit risks, you can find bargains. This increases the new lessor's operating margins.

Reinvestment.   Aggressive cash flow reinvestment is also a requirement for this type of fund. Sometimes debt is used but not too much, because it will dilute the level of cash distributions to investors. Financial advisors should look for greater subordination from leasing fund sponsors, if an aggressive reinvestment strategy is pursued by the fund's management. It is only logical because if the sponsor tells the investor that more cash must be used to acquire more equipment for growth of the program, then the sponsor should also be more willing to subordinate his own operating fees to the backend of the program.

Vendor Leasing.   As noted, vendor leasing programs allow discounts for the lessor on the purchase of the equipment by his working as the lease financing arm of a manufacturer. It is important, however, that fund management avoid placing too much activity with a single vendor. Sponsors should be specific about how much they will commit to a particular manufacturer. A good rule of thumb is to limit fund investment to less than 20, even 10 percent, in any single equipment manufacturer.

Conservative Lease Structure

It is advisable that these funds adopt a conservative leasing structure. If they attempt to make their money through credit risk management and aggressive used (or new) equipment acquisition, then these funds should aim to balance investor protection by avoiding the added risk of operating lease activity.

12

Venture Leasing Funds

Venture leasing funds are a new idea wrapped in a fairly old concept. In recent years, several equipment leasing public fund sponsors have essentially adapted the financial techniques of venture capitalism to the business of equipment leasing.

The aim of these venture leasing funds is to acquire equipment for lease primarily to development or start-up stage companies that promise potentially high financial rewards to the lessor. The investment objectives of these funds include:

- High cash yields from the leasing activity

- Warrants or equity kickers from the start-up lessees to provide the potential of substantial returns if the new company is successful

- Protect limited partner investments through primary use of full-payout leases

- Partial tax shelter during the early years of the venture leasing program

How Venture Leasing Works

A start-up venture needs equipment to begin operations, but without much of an operating history, these entrepreneurs find traditional financing sources hard to attract. Leasing their basic equipment—rather than buying the equipment—often provides a good solution to both its credit and cash flow situation. But the price is not cheap.

Such a start-up or early stage company must pay high enough equipment rentals to offset the threat of default. For this reason, start-up companies will also avoid financing through leasing firms that require high upfront cash escrow deposits or lease commitment fees that can be as much as 50 to 70 percent of the original equipment cost.

In return for a couple of percentage points off the lease rate, a venture leasing firm will take stock warrants in the fledgling company. If that new company becomes successful (there are always different levels of success) either through a public stock offer or leveraged buyout or through aquisition or refinancing, the venture lessor stands to make a great deal of profit on the deal. Venture capitalists and venture lessors call such successes *homeruns*. Here's one example from the files of the operator of venture leasing funds:

In Februrary of 1986, a maker of microcomputer boards leased $400,000 worth of various production equipment from the venture lessor. In July of 1987, the venture leasing partnership sold off 11,900 stock warrants that it had obtained in the original lease agreement with the start-up. That stock sale produced net profit of $275,000 for the venture lessor. But during the 18 months of the lease agreement, the leasing fund was also earning 15 percent a year in lease income, or another $90,000 in just a year-and-a-half. The leasing fund also holds an additional block of warrants that was worth $810,000 in July 1987. In roughly two years, the fund will have recovered its original investment and stands to gain substantially more on continuing lease rentals on the full-payout lease and anticipates further stock equity payoffs down the line.

Understanding Venture Capitalism

It is important to understand how venture capitalism works to appreciate the potential risks and rewards of venture leasing.

Venture capital is dominated by a group of some 200 investment companies that fund most of the start-ups and early stage companies in the U.S. These financiers are a mix of high-rollers and institutional investors who focus largely on the high-tech companies near Silicon Valley and Route 128 west of Boston. These venture capital firms provide funding at different stages of the startup of a firm. These stages include seed money for establishment of a business concept, first-round financing for initial manufacturing and tooling, and second round or mezzanine financing for a major capital expansion to get the firm off and producing money.

These venturesome investors look for high rewards. The industry looks for the return of capital of at least eight times its original investment over a seven-year period, with average annual returns of about 38 percent. But such returns are necessary because so many of the startups flop. The average of homeruns among the startups is slim. For every venture-backed successs such as Apple Computer, another nine fail.

What holds true for the venture capitalist holds true for those engaged in venture leasing. It is a highly speculative leasing fund investment that is not for the anxious limited partner investor. There is also a problem because these funds are so new. Not one of them has gone full-cycle and while anecdotal success stories make for great press releases, they do not assure ultimate returns.

Evaluating Venture Leasing Funds

In addition to knowing how to manage equipment under lease, the venture lessor had better know something about the venture capital business. This experience does not come easily in an investment community that is so close knit and where the successful deals are few and far between. Very often, learning about the good deals is a matter of who you know, because the venture financiers often share risk with their colleagues by doling out portions of their investment with a like-minded group of backers.

The important issue is being able to judge promising companies and the nature of a variety of high-tech industries in which most of the start-ups try to enter play. Again, this knowledge does not grow on trees. Does the venture leasing firm's management have this kind of experience? It needs to be demontrated by a track record.

Some due diligence analysts of these venture leasing funds believe that the venture risk dilutes the leasing income of the partnership. There is no easy way to properly evaluate this criticism except to be prudent about fund financial projections. For example, warrants or equity kickers, while possible, should not be included in the investor's potential cash projections. The projections should stand on the leasing activity alone. If a sweet deal come up, so much the better, but it is unhealthy to go beyond lease rental income and conservative residual values in investor projections.

Equipment risk should be minimized. The fund should primarily invest in standard types of equipment with strong remarketing potential and residual predictability. Equipment that would fall into this category would be basic testing and production equipment or other equipment essential to the operation. In other words, the equipment leased to the start-up firm should be so essential to survival that to default would mean the company could not exist. It would also mean that should the firm default, a healthy market should exist for the release or sale of the equipment.

The venture leasing firm should use primarily full-payout leases which aim to recover all original equipment cost under the initial term of the lease. However, this does not mean that the venture lessor should accept low rental rates. Many typical lease rates to start-up firms aim for as much as a 3.5 percent net monthly lease rate. The usual breakeven on these leases averages between 19 and 24 months—that is, the period required for the rents and residual to cover 100 percent of original equipment cost and lessor overhead.

Venture lessors usually look for warrants and kickers worth a minimum of 15 percent of the original cost of the leased equipment. Some analysts would look for even more because of the nature of the risks involved. In other words, if a venture deal is so risky, an investor needs potentially explosive returns such as the traditional venture capital firms require as basic investment criteria. A 38 percent annual cash return looks much more attractive to a high roller than a 10 to 15 percent cash return that venture leasing firms say they anticipate.

Some sponsors liken venture leasing fund investments to going to the race track, but with a guarantee. To these promoters, it is like betting on a long shot (the venture risk), but still getting your bet back (in the form of lease rentals.) That may be true but you still have to bet on the right horse, and as far as the fund limited partner is concerned, the right horse is the general partner who is supposed to be running this horse race.

Ask for the Facts

Financial advisors and potential investors in venture leasing funds need to be assured of the skills of the general partner. This should mean more than anecdotal evidence of an occasional home run on a particular lease transaction.

We recommend that advisors ask the sponsor to spell out venture leasing activity. This would include a complete inventory of leases, lessees, lease cash returns on each, warrants negotiated and exercised, if any, duration of transaction, default rates, release, and remarketing experience for each lease. This may sound lengthy and in some other partnerships may be overkill, but venture leasing promises need to be quantified. If a sponsor balks at this, ask him or her: would you lease to a company that has nothing but promises to offer? Wouldn't the lessor also want to see all the facts, including financial statements and prior management performance?

The last suggestion is that only the most stout-hearted investors seek out venture leasing funds. They are risky. No one should be deceived about that. Investors should diversify these kinds of risks with a range of other investments, including perhaps more predictable equipment leasing partnerships that focus more heavily on capital protection.

13

Lease Option Funds

It should be clear that residual risk management is the key to the success of any equipment leasing partnership. How the residual risk is structured determines in large measure how the leasing fund operates. It is also true that institutional lenders and lessors dominate the U.S. leasing business. These two facts of the equipment leasing business have led to the emergence of a new type of leasing fund which we call *lease options*.

So far the concept of equipment lease option funds has only surfaced in privately offered programs. It is likely, however, that these types of funds, properly structured, will find wider attraction in the public limited partnership market. How do they work?

Lease Option Concept

Institutional lenders and lessors are primarily financial operations. The large majority of equipment leasing is done through direct finance leasing (full-payout leases) arrangements between major corporations and major lenders. These lenders and lessors are not risk-takers. Their aim is to lend money—leasing is just another financing scheme as far as they are concerned. These large portfolio lenders are not interested in remarketing the equipment or in betting on the residual of any equipment. Institutional lessors are simply not in the equipment business.

In addition, under Regulation Y of the Federal Reserve Banking Regulations, bank holding companies have not been permitted to take more than a 20 percent residual (or 25 percent residual through a subsidiary) on equipment under lease. In effect, this means that the bank can show that an asset is worth only one-fifth of the purchase price of equipment regardless of what the equipment will really be worth when the lease ends. The result is that much of the equipment in the bank's leasing portfolio may be undervalued on the bank's books. This is the lease option opportunity.

What the managers of a lease options fund will now do is investigate these equipment assets and make an offer to the institutional lender. The process goes something like this:

1. The would-be option holder obtains third-party appraisals of the equipment in the institution's portfolio, particularly large equipment, such as aircraft, barges, railroad locomotives, and other equipment that represents a hefty exposure for the institution.
2. The option seeker will then offer the institutional lessor a fixed sum of money today for the right to participate in the proceeds of the sale of the equipment above a set price—called the *strike price*—when the lease expires.

Here's an illustration of an option deal. Let's assume that an institutional lessor has bought a commercial jet airplane for $20 million and leased it to a major airline. Under banking regulations, the institution can list the value of the aircraft at no more than 20 percent of the purchase price, or $4 million, when the lease ends in five years.

This airplane is appraised by independent experts to have a residual value of somewhere between $8 to 12 million five years hence. The option seeker might then offer the bank lessor $400,000 today for the right to participate in 50 percent of the residual value in excess of $6.5 million. How does this break out for the parties?

The institution is satisfied because it gets $400,000 today which it happily books as ordinary income. It has reduced its exposure to the equipment. The income received has not cost the institutional lessor anything because the book value of the equipment is still $4 million. From the option holder's viewpoint, he calculates the future value of the $400,000 to be somewhere between $700,000 and $800,000 in five years based on various discount rate assumptions.

Analyzing the Option

Analyzing the option, let's assume the actual residual value of the airplane when it comes off lease in five years is at the low, worst case appraisal, or $8 million. In this case, the option holder has the right to share in 50 percent of the excess of the recovery over the strike price of $6.5 million, or 50 percent of $1.5 million = $750,000. This return to the option holder provides both the recovery of the original $400,000 plus provides a yield ($350,000) that is roughly equal to his assumed discount rate of his cash investment five years ago. This is the worst case scenario if the option holder has played all his cards conservatively.

Now assume that the aircraft is sold at the moderate to high side of the original residual estimate. If the airplane is sold for $10 million, the option holder shares 50 percent of $3.5 million and receives $1.75 million. If sold at the high side of the residual appraisal, the option holder nets $2.75 million ($12 million - $6.5 million = $5.5 million × .5 = $2.75 million.)

In our moderate-to-best-case residual scenario, the option holder is looking at a net return of $1.75 million to $2.75 million in five years compared to an original investment of $400,000.

Lease option fund managers expect substantial rewards with even low-side residual activity. On an annual basis, one such estimate indicated returns can range from a low of about 2.5 times the cash investment over nine years (or an internal rate of return of about 15%) to a high-side estimate of 4.5 to 5.5 times cash investment, or about a 35 percent IRR.

These IRR estimates, according to the sponsors of these lease options funds, do not include estimates for inflation, another conservative approach. If, for example, one assumes a 5 percent inflation factor over the nine-year life of this lease option limited partnership, there would be an additional return of about 250 percent for the partnership.

Diversifying Some Risks

It sounds almost too good to be true. But it should be obvious that everything hinges on the residual bet. To reduce other associated risks, the equipment picked for the options portfolio are mixed by type to avoid putting too many assets in one industry basket. In addition, these funds attempt to stagger maturities of the options over a number of years. These funds also aim to have the institutional lessor remarket the equipment on the back end of the lease. This does a couple of things.

If the institutional lender is sharing in the residual proceeds, the incentive is to get the most for the equipment at the end of the lease. It also allows the option holder the cost advantage of not attempting to handle the remarketing on his own.

Promoters of these new lease option funds see enormous potential if they can prove the concept, which is still too new for any real track record. The lion's share of the $100 billion U.S. equipment leasing industry each year is arranged through institutional sources to only the best customers from the Fortune 500 list. This is a marketplace that is relatively untapped by equipment leasing partnerships and provides enormous potential for future growth.

By providing a means for individuals to participate in residual proceeds with major lessors and institutions, individual limited partners are able to gain access to a very attractive investment market.

Another attraction from a corporate lessee's standpoint is that the lease option may provide lower lease rates to the lessee. If the lease option proves successful and is introduced into the original lease agreement at the start, it will have the competitive effect of lowering initial lease rates.

Some Caveats

At this writing, the lease option partnership has not been approved for public sale by the Securities and Exchange Commission (SEC). This does not indicate anything wrong with the concept, only that the SEC must hold hearings and investigate the various aspects of what is a very new concept.

Initial sales in private offerings have been highly attractive to individual and institutional partnership investors. Thus, it is likely that the concept will appear in the public marketplace. And here is where the difficulties might enter.

As we've stressed, the entire bet hinges on the residual estimate and the target strike price negotiated by the option seeker. If residual appraisals are done haphazardly or optimistically, the clear danger to the investor is that he will be buying a worthless piece of paper. It is thus extremely important that the public offering specify the equipment and strike prices to be offered during at least the initial operation of the fund. The criteria for option buys should be clearly spelled out in detail. Discount rate assumptions should be conservative.

And what is the experience of the lease option fund's general partner? Has the management worked extensively with institutional lessors and in the equipment leasing business? Are multiple residual appraisals offered for evaluation? What are the credentials of the appraisers?

Investor suitability, as always, is a key factor in the recommendation of one of these option funds. It is especially important to understand that this is a bet on a residual outcome many years down the road. The fund itself has very limited control over its destiny—it is not actively engaged in the remarketing of the equipment, but must rely on the institution to do that job.

All of these caveats indicate the downside risks of this type of investment. This is true with any investment, but these funds do represent a new, and perhaps promising, option for those interested in the equipment leasing marketplace.

14

Leasing Fund Trends

The equipment leasing partnership market has grown quickly in just the past few years. But where is it headed? What are the dominant trends for equipment leasing in general? Will the market see the introduction of more hybrid forms of leasing funds, such as venture leasing or lease options?

No leasing market observer is blessed with any greater insight than another, but some trends are emerging and stabilizing. In this chapter we will try to identify these trends and suggest future directions. But one element is fairly clear: the move away from tax-oriented leasing will continue to benefit leasing partnerships that provide high current income.

Liquidity

There have been a few attempts to provide liquidity in some leasing funds in recent years, but the issue is unsettled. The primary vehicle for providing liquidity for partnership investors has been the application of master limited partnerships (MLPs).

MLPs were developed in 1982 in the oil and gas partnership market. The idea then was to roll up the assets of several oil drilling partnerships into a single entity that would trade in a public market. In 1987, several equipment leasing fund sponsors took the MLP concept and packaged it for investor consumption. In one case, assets from previous partnerships managed by the sponsor were rolled up into a single master limited partnership whose units were intended to be traded on the New York Stock Exchange at some future date. In another instance, an aircraft leasing partnership was offered with the exclusive intent of trading on the public market once the initial partnership offering closed for subscription. In yet another instance, a sponsor of a diversified transportation fund offered investors the possibility of listing on a major exchange some two years after the initial partnership offering closed.

These attempts proved temporarily attractive. But the problem is that the entire concept is under attack by the Internal Revenue Service which has argued, along with some influential members of Congress, that MLPs should be taxed as corporations. The issue of liquidity for limited partnerships, in the minds of the IRS and others, is what determines the nature of a taxable corporate entity. The mood of tax reform and efforts to increase federal revenue have effectively tabled the rush to master limited partnership activities. The future of MLPs—for leasing or other partnerships—looks remote because once these partnerships are subject to corporate taxation their attraction will dissolve almost completely. In 1988, as if to demonstrate the demise of the MLP, the entire market plummeted at the uncertainty of IRS and congressional intentions.

But the promise of liquidity for partnerships is still attractive to many investors. This probably explains development of secondary markets for limited partnership units, including some equipment leasing funds still in their early operating stages. The difficulty with these secondary markets, at least for the leasing fund unit holders, is that they are almost always sold at deep discounts. Some broker/dealers have made an active little market for these limited partner shares.

The real issue for investors is to ask if liquidity suits investments that are intended to be long-term, fixed investments. The author's feeling is that long-term leasing investments are not designed to provide liquidity. The specter of IRS double-taxation does not sweeten the idea. If one wants to trade in limited partnership units, then he or she can play on the secondary markets. Why invest in a partnership at the front-end, pay for 15 to 20 percent front-end fees, and hope for a favorable response on the public market when the investor would do immeasurably better by buying deeply discounted limited partnership units on the secondary market? Our belief is that attempts to create liquidity for partnership units have been a sales scheme more than a true investor alternative. It has been a trendy sort of idea whose attraction was emotional and not geared to any fundamental investment logic.

Computer Equipment

For several years now, the author has heard rumblings from numerous partnership sponsors, broker/dealers, due diligence experts, and financial advisors about the glut of computer leasing funds on the public partnership market. The complaint, never systematically proved, is that these funds, many of recent vintage, are forcing lease rentals too low or are being managed by inexperienced general partners. The combination of low initial rentals and weak ability to remarket the computer equipment is expected to doom many of these funds in upcoming years when the full results of the fund's long-term prospects begin to emerge.

There is no way short of a longer tracking period to determine if these fears are justified. Our suspicion is that some of these funds will collapse. How many? We don't know. What does this bode for new computer leasing funds? Are lease rentals being driven down too low by the competitive pressures of these funds chasing too few prospective lessees? We do not know. But it is likely the growth of equipment leasing partnerships may follow the pattern that developed in the real estate partnership market. In the 1970s and early 1980s, real estate partnerships soared and then collapsed when many of the funds ran into trouble. Much of the trouble then was due to get-rich-quick wholesalers who were peddling promises rather than managing the real estate assets properly. After a useful shakeout, however, the real estate partnership business rebounded. The same pattern may also emerge in equipment leasing.

What has become clear in the growth of the limited partnership market, including equipment leasing funds, is that the investor is investing in a company, not just a pile of rocks or a heap of gadgets which somehow magically throw off cash. Any fixed asset investment—real estate, oil and gas, or equipment leasing—is really a business that must be operated for profit. We hope we have made this point amply clear. The performance of the fund is directly contingent on able general partner management.

Miscellaneous Funds

This understanding that partnerships are operating businesses has led to the growth of a whole category of funds that defy easy classification. Industry rating services call these funds miscellaneous or other. They resemble equipment leasing funds in that the investor bets on the successful management of specific assets by the fund manager. Sometimes they involve leasing, such as venture leasing funds, but most often they might fund a new product introduction or leveraged buyouts or a dairy business or a video rental business or the list is endless.

What we're pointing out is that limited partnerships provide a means of raising capital for many businesses, including equipment leasing. The fundamental issue is not the assets themselves, but how they are managed. In that sense, equipment leasing funds have changed the outlook on the entire limited partnership industry. The value of partnerships—no double-taxation like a corporation and the ability to allocate different partner interests—provide advantages over corporate stock.

Mix and Match Partner Shares

Limited partnership interests can be split into different classifications to suit different types of investors. This can be done in leasing partnerships, too. Partnership tax law permits flexibility in the allocation of income, gain, loss, or deductions among the partners. For example, splitting an equipment leasing investment into current income, deferred income, and growth units can attract both institutional and individual investors. For example, one class of investor may have priority claims on leasing fund cash flow while a special interest partner (say an institutional investor) would be allocated the bulk of taxable losses. So far, the direct participation marketplace has not put this flexibility of partnerships into wider use. But it does provide an alternative to traditional stock financing. If a partnership can avoid double taxation, pass through depreciation to other entities, and create limited liability for different classes of income treatment, then the idea may provide an advantage to investors with a variety of interests.

New Equipment Trends

Theoretically, any piece of equipment can be leased. For the leasing fund, however, only certain types of equipment can provide the opportunities for significant cash flow that the investment requires. One area of growth appears to be telecommunications equipment. This is a potentially enormous area of equipment growth.

Advances in technology, like fiber optics and superconductivity, are transforming the traditional means of business data processing and communication. The breakup of the Bell System and the deregulation of the communications industry is setting off a dramatic spurt of technology investment in telecommunications. Some of this equipment is being leased through partnerships. The future is bright for this equipment category, but many leasing firms are only beginning to understand the dynamics of the telecommunications market. Residual expectations are extremely difficult to quantify. But the growth of the entire telecommunications industry is certain to provide new opportunities for leasing funds in the future.

Co-generation equipment is another area of possible leasing growth. These systems promise utility users, such as hospitals, factories, and other major consumers, lower power generation costs. One difficulty is that the new tax law extended the depreciation life of co-generation equipment to 15 years which limits its ability to shelter leasing cash flow. But it is a promising technology for lessors nonetheless.

Manufacturers as Fund Sponsors

As we've mentioned, many major manufacturers engage in their own equipment leasing activities through captive leasing subsidiaries. Like any other financing operation, these leasing entities of manufacturers must raise money to finance the business. Why not go into the syndication business themselves?

Just such activity is emerging. In one case, a major computer division of McDonnell Douglas has formed a leasing partnership with the express purpose of financing its leasing activities, at least in part, through funds raised in a public limited partnership. In another case, General Electric Credit Corporation has acquired majority control of

Polaris Aircraft, a leading sponsor of aircraft leasing partnerships. Ford Motor Company acquired control of a major leasing firm, U.S. Leasing, which also sponsors equipment leasing partnerships. It is difficult to guess the depth of this interest of major equipment makers in the leasing partnership business. It may only be incidental. But it may provide new opportunities for investors to share more directly in the operations of these major players.

The great advantage of equipment leasing over ownership is its flexibility. This accounts for the dramatic growth of leasing in the first place and encourages future prospects for the leasing funds business, too. But while the equipment and structure of the leasing partnership may change, the underlying economics of the investment still must be established. This is the aim of Part III of this book: how to analyze equipment leasing partnerships.

III
Analyzing Leasing Partnerships

15
Yield Analysis

One current leasing handbook lists more than two dozen methods to calculate yields on leased equipment. There are no lack of means to analyze equipment leasing, including a variety of payback and net present value techniques. But efforts to quantity returns on leasing fund partnerships but can be very misleading for those who recommend or buy these investments. The key is to assess the underlying assumptions behind the numbers.

Techniques such as internal rate of return or modified rate of return calculations do not yield magic numbers. These projections are of little value if they are based on unlikely assumptions that neither match the history of the fund sponsor nor the economics of the equipment.

In this chapter we will present ways to judge the operating assumptions of the leasing fund as well as the projected return to the investor.

Evaluating Operating Assumptions

Evaluating an equipment leasing fund investment is like sizing up any business operation. What are the primary assumptions of the business operation? How likely are these predictions to become reality? What is the strength of the management or business plan? How realistic are key leasing assumptions concerning lease rental incomes and residual values? These kinds of questions go to the heart of any presentation of possible outcomes.

Figures 15.1 and 15.2 are sample projections of a container

leasing fund. Figure 15.1 details lease operating projections and 15.2 shows after-tax projections for the limited partnership. They are good examples of fund operating projections, because they provide a level of detail that permits a better evaluation of the fund's business plan. These projections also permit us to show how the key variables influence the outcome of equipment leasing fund activity.

The sample fund used in Figures 15.1 and 15.2 is a $30 million leasing partnership that is to invest primarily in marine containers. The base case, or mid-range operating scenario, is shown. This base case projected a 15.1 percent pretax internal rate of return and an 11.6 percent after-tax return. A low case and an upside case was also developed by the sponsors. But how are these projections determined?

Key Assumptions

The projections make key operating assumptions. These assumptions are what produce the numbers. We need to go behind the numbers. The heart of the yield evaluation by the financial advisor and investor is to probe the likelihood of these assumptions. The key assumptions fall into a few broad categories, starting with how the investors' contributions (fund proceeds) are to be used. Next, several assumptions were made about the key operating variables. Further assumptions were made about management fees, investor tax rates, timing of equipment purchases, depreciation, and interest earned on cash balances.

Use of Proceeds

Industry guidelines pretty much set the range of offering cost fees and sales commissions. But these front-end costs can effectively range between 11 and 22 percent of the investor's initial contribution. That is a big difference. A key disadvantage of any limited partnership is the relatively high level of front-end costs. You cannot avoid this fact of business, but the difference between an 11 and 22 percent upfront cost is not small. It further indicates the willingness of the partner to defer some of these fees to later stages of the program, when it is better tied to fund management performance through incentive fees.

Figure 15.1
Lease Operating Projections (Due Diligence Base Case—TCC Equipment Income Fund 1 September 1987)

	Year 1	Year 2	Year 3	Year 4	Year 5	Year 6	Year 7	Year 8
CASH DISTRIBUTIONS								
Rental Revenue ($)	1,878,329	7,927,238	8,123,722	8,535,036	9,133,798	9,812,316	10,541,548	11,420,537
Interest Income	227,740	197,344	55,315	206,277	217,669	240,345	255,626	293,758
Total Revenue	2,106,068	8,124,582	8,179,036	8,741,313	9,351,466	10,052,661	10,797,174	11,714,295
Less:								
Storage Expense	62,222	260,251	340,325	369,584	395,511	424,892	456,470	494,531
Other Operating Expense	314,751	1,316,491	1,370,321	1,467,155	1,570,081	1,686,717	1,812,071	1,963,167
Total Operating Expense	376,972	1,576,742	1,710,646	1,836,739	1,965,593	2,111,610	2,268,540	2,457,699
Gross Operating Margin	1,729,096	6,547,841	6,468,390	6,904,574	7,385,874	7,941,051	8,528,634	9,256,596
Less:								
Management Fees	131,483	554,907	690,703	843,912	885,826	1,104,118	1,163,145	1,237,097
Debt Interest Expense	0	0	0	0	(0)	(0)	(1)	(1)
Debt Principal Payment	0	0	0	3	1	1	1	1
Net Operating Margin	1,495,317	5,565,067	5,777,687	6,060,658	6,500,048	6,836,933	7,365,489	8,025,842
Plus Container Sales Proceeds	0	0	0	0	0	0	0	0
Cash From Operations	1,597,613	5,992,934	5,777,687	6,060,658	6,500,048	6,836,933	7,365,489	8,025,842
Less:								
Gen. Partner Unsubord. Distr	74,766	189,474	189,474	197,368	205,263	213,158	213,158	401,292
General Partner Subord.	0	0	0	0	0	0	0	0
Total GP	74,766	189,474	189,474	197,368	205,263	213,158	213,158	401,292
LIMITED PARTNER DISTRIBUTION								
Amount ($)	1,420,551	3,600,000	3,600,000	3,750,001	3,900,001	4,050,001	4,050,001	7,624,550
% Original Investment	6.9	12.0	12.0	12.5	13.0	13.5	13.5	25.4
Reinvested in Equipment	102,296	2,203,460	1,988,213	2,113,289	2,394,784	2,573,774	3,102,330	0
IRR 15.1%								

Continued next page

Figure 15.1
Lease Operating Projections (continued)

	Year 9	Year 10	Year 11	Year 12	Year 13	Year 14	Year 15	Year 16
CASH DISTRIBUTIONS								
Rental Revenue ($)	11,420,537	11,420,537	11,420,537	11,420,537	11,420,537	7,617,498	3,814,459	0
Interest Income	126,387	123,781	123,742	123,626	123,152	122,643	159,474	118,639
Total Revenue	11,546,924	11,544,318	11,544,279	11,544,163	11,543,689	7,740,142	3,973,933	118,639
Less:								
Storage Expense	494,531	494,531	494,531	494,531	494,531	329,853	165,174	0
Other Operating Expense	1,963,167	1,963,167	1,963,167	1,963,167	1,963,167	1,309,433	655,698	0
Total Operating Expense	2,457,699	2,457,699	2,457,699	2,457,699	2,457,699	1,639,285	820,871	0
Gross Operating Margin	9,089,225	9,086,620	9,086,581	9,086,464	9,085,991	6,100,857	3,153,062	118,639
Less:								
Management Fees	1,237,097	1,237,097	1,244,800	1,276,272	1,309,723	1,081,481	855,946	638,041
Debt Interest Expense	(1)	(1)	(1)	(1)	(1)	(1)	(1)	(1)
Debt Principal Payment	0	0	0	0	0	0	0	0
Net Operating Margin	7,852,129	7,849,523	7,841,782	7,810,194	7,776,268	5,019,440	2,297,117	(519,401)
Plus Container Sales Proceeds	0	0	0	0	0	5,212,199	5,212,199	5,227,852
Cash From Operations	7,852,129	7,849,523	7,841,782	7,810,194	7,776,268	10,231,639	7,509,317	4,708,451
Less:								
Gen. Partner Unsubord. Distr	392,606	392,476	392,089	390,510	388,813	511,582	375,466	235,423
General Partner Subord.	0	466,360	784,178	781,019	777,627	1,023,164	750,932	470,845
Total GP	392,606	858,836	1,176,267	1,171,529	1,166,440	1,534,746	1,126,397	706,268
LIMITED PARTNER DISTRIBUTION								
Amount ($)	7,459,552	6,990,687	6,665,514	6,638,665	6,609,828	8,696,893	6,382,919	4,002,183
% Original Investment	24.9	23.3	22.2	22.1	22.0	29.0	21.3	13.3
Reinvested in Equipment	0	0	0	(0)	0	0	0	0
IRR 15.1%								

Source: Textainer Capital Corporation

Figure 15.2
After-Tax Fund Projections (Due Diligence Base Case—TCC Equipment Income Fund 1 September 1987)

	Year 1	Year 2	Year 3	Year 4	Year 5	Year 6	Year 7	Year 8
TAX CONSEQUENCES								
Cash From Operations ($)	1,495,317	5,565,067	5,777,687	6,060,658	6,500,048	6,836,933	7,365,489	8,025,842
Plus Principal Payments	0	0	0	3	1	1	1	1
Less Depreciation	2,595,001	4,608,168	4,689,268	5,020,640	5,372,855	5,771,987	3,605,949	2,109,837
Less Front End Fees	0	0	0	0	0	0	0	0
Taxable Income (Loss)	(1,099,684)	956,899	1,088,420	1,040,022	1,127,193	1,064,947	3,759,541	5,916,006
Ltd. Partner Share Tax. Inc.	(1,044,700)	909,054	1,033,999	988,021	1,070,834	1,011,699	3,571,564	5,620,206
Loss Carry Forward	(1,044,700)	(135,646)	0	0	0	0	0	0
Adj. Ltd. Tax. Income	0	0	898,353	988,021	1,070,834	1,011,699	3,571,564	5,620,206
Ltd. Tax. Pat.	0	0	296,456	326,047	353,375	333,861	1,178,616	1,854,668
LTD AFTER TAX CASH DIST	$1,420,551	$3,600,000	$3,303,544	$3,423,954	$3,546,625	$3,716,140	$2,871,384	$5,769,882
% Original Invest.	4.7	12.0	11.0	11.4	11.8	12.4	9.6	19.2
IRR 11.5%								
UNITS IN FLEET								
20'	1390	2469	2512	2690	2878	3092	3322	3599
40'	1877	3333	3392	3632	3886	4175	4485	4859
Chassis	593	1053	1072	1148	1228	1319	1417	1536
Reefer	111	197	201	215	230	247	266	288
Hi Cube	618	1097	1116	1195	1279	1374	1476	1600
Tanks	62	110	112	120	128	137	148	160
Total	4651	8260	8405	8999	9630	10346	11114	12041

Continued on next page

Figure 15.2
After-Tax Fund Projections (continued)

	Year 9	Year 10	Year 11	Year 12	Year 13	Year 14	Year 15	Year 16
TAX CONSEQUENCES								
Cash From Operations ($)	7,852,129	7,849,523	7,841,782	7,810,194	7,776,268	10,231,639	7,509,317	4,708,451
Plus Principal Payments	0	0	0	0	0	0	0	0
Less Depreciation	2,028,737	1,697,367	1,345,151	946,019	517,056	0	0	0
Less Front End Fees	0	0	0	0	0	0	0	3,540,000
Taxable Income (Loss)	5,823,392	6,152,156	6,496,630	6,864,174	7,259,212	10,231,639	7,509,317	1,168,451
Ltd. Partner Share Tax. Inc.	5,532,222	5,479,033	5,522,136	5,834,548	6,170,330	8,696,893	6,382,919	993,183
Loss Carry Forward	0	0	0	0	0	0	0	0
Adj. Ltd. Tax. Income	5,532,222	5,479,033	5,522,136	5,834,548	6,170,330	8,696,893	6,382,919	993,183
Ltd. Tax. Pat.	1,825,633	1,808,081	1,822,305	1,925,401	2,036,209	2,869,975	2,106,363	327,750
LTD AFTER TAX CASH DIST	$5,633,889	$5,182,606	$4,843,209	$4,713,264	$4,573,619	$5,826,918	$4,276,556	$3,674,433
% Original Invest.	18.8	17.3	16.1	15.7	15.2	19.4	14.3	12.2
IRR 11.5%								
UNITS IN FLEET								
20'	3599	3599	3599	3599	3599	2400	1202	0
40'	4859	4859	4859	4859	4859	3241	1623	0
Chassis	1536	1536	1536	1536	1536	1024	513	0
Reefer	288	288	288	288	288	192	96	0
Hi Cube	1600	1600	1600	1600	1600	1067	534	0
Tanks	160	160	160	160	160	107	53	0
Total	12041	12041	12041	12041	12041	8031	4022	0

Source: Textainer Capital Corporation

In our sample case, a total front-end load of 16.3 percent is projected, of which 9 percent went to sales commissions, 2.8 percent for offering and organizational expenses, 4.2 percent as management fees for acquiring the equipment, and 0.3 percent for a working capital reserve. This means that 83.7 percent or $25,105,000 of the $30 million raised through the limited partners' investment went into the leasing program—referred to as the *percent in property.*

Operating Variables

Imbedded in the sample projections are the key assumptions about the leasing fund's operation, in this case: equipment mix and price, lease rates, equipment utilization, operating expenses, and residual values. If, for example, you look at rental revenues for the first 5 years of the 16 years of the program's expected life, you see rents and effective lease rate factors of:

Year	Revenue	Effective annual lease rates
1	$ 1,878,329	7.48 %
2	7,927,238	31.57
3	8,123,722	32.35
4	8,535,036	33.99
5	9,133,798	36.37

How are these rentals derived? The sponsor has developed a rental revenue model based on equipment utilization and expected lease rates per equipment unit per day. In the sponsor's due diligence memoranda, he has detailed these rentals for specific types of equipment—standard dry containers, refrigerated containers, etc.—based on the target percentages of equipment to be acquired by the fund. In this base case, the equipment mix will be: standard dry containers (40-foot) = 35 percent of investment; 20-foot dry containers (15 percent); refrigerated containers (15 percent), chassis containers (10 percent), high cube containers (15 percent), and tank containers (10 percent). The sponsor has likewise included equipment rental rates and equipment utilization factors for each type of container.

In this case, the leasing sponsor fund is projecting equipment utilization of 80 to 85 percent for the standard dry containers, 90 to

100 percent for the tank and refrigerated containers and 80 to 85 percent for the chassis and high cube containers. Are these assumptions reasonable? The recent history of the sponsor's utilization rate exceeds 90 percent. Industry averages are within the 80 to 85 percent range. So we have some basis for this assumption.

How do the sponsor's projected rental rates compare with the industry's recent norms? Average daily rates—the standard measure of container leasing rates—for the industry range from $1.20 to $1.50 for 20-feet dry containers and from $2.30 to $2.65 for 40-foot containers. These standard containers raise additional revenue by as much as $0.30 per day for dropoff charges, pickup charges, handling, insurance, and repair charges. Using these figures we can compare industry norms to the base case projection of the sponsor:

Equipment type	Average daily rental rates	
	Sponsor	Industry
40-ft	$ 2.75-2.95	$2.60-2.95
20-ft	1.65-1.75	1.50-1.80

So it appears that the sponsor's rental projections are in line with industry norms and expectations. We are not suggesting that all financial advisors have the time to ferret out all the industry operating norms for the particular equipment under lease. But the sponsor's projections need to be compared to reality—both in terms of the industry's history and expectation and through the sponsor's prior operating and fund performance.

General partner management fees average about 7 percent in this fund and follow partnership guidelines established by the North American Securities Administrators Association (NASAA). The sponsor projects operating expenses that range between 20 and 24 percent of revenues. These ongoing expenses are compatible with other competitive leasing funds. Projections in Figure 15.1 incorporate these ongoing operating expenses.

Residual Assumptions

In this model from the sponsor, residual values for each type of equipment have also been included. For this base case, the following residual values have been projected:

Equipment type	Original cost	Residual value	Residual percentage
40-ft	$ 2,765	$ 1,200	43%
20-ft	1,600	800	50
Refrigerated	20,000	6,000	30
Chassis	2,500	1,200	48
High cube	3,600	1,200	33
Tanks	24,000	8,000	33

How do these residual assumptions compare to industry and sponsor history? Most standard containers have a primary economic life of between 9 and 14 years. A long history of 50 percent residuals has been established. Stronger manufacturing construction has also improved the durability of the containers and thus the economic life of the equipment. With standard construction, the containers are unlikely to become obsolete. There is also a steady rate of retirement of containers, of about 200,000 a year. Users also pay for damage to the equipment during transit and regular inspections of the equipment before and after lease help ensure that the equipment is not subject to poor handling. It becomes clear when these factors are considered that the expected residual projections by the sponsor are conservative.

In addition, the sponsor has further reduced the impact of residual values on expected fund performance by a couple of important strategies. First, the fund will not begin selling the equipment until the 14th year of the program. This longer life (versus 5 to 12 years on many leasing partnerships) reduces the impact of residual assumptions on overall returns. For example, by changing the residual assumptions from 50 to 20 percent, the impact on pretax returns in the best case scenario was marginal, dropping from 16.6 percent to only 15.3 percent.

In general, equipment leasing partnerships project annual cash-on-cash returns of between 10 to 20 percent over the life of the program. Such cash distributions are necessary to induce investors to choose leasing partnerships over less risky alternative fixed investments in bonds or government backed securities. Aside from leasing partnerships that invest primarily in computer equipment (where risks are highest), there is little correlation between expected returns and the type of equipment acquired for the lease investment. However, in evaluating projected yields, it is necessary to compare key assumptions on lease rates and residual values for the specific equipment under lease. Figures 6.1 and 8.2 provide a range of norms by equipment type for these underlying lease fund assumptions. Perhaps even more important is how these projections by the sponsor compare to that sponsor's past operating history in obtaining target lease rates and residual values.

Reinvestment Assumptions

The sponsor of this sample fund has also set out a reinvestment strategy to increase fund assets over the life of the program. The sponsor has the option to use up to 25 percent debt to acquire bargain-priced equipment that might become available, but this is not included in the operating projections. The fund manager plans to reinvest all cash flow above the 12 percent investor distribution in new equipment during the first seven years of the program.

Is this reinvestment plan too high, too low, or about right? There is no certain way to judge the right amount of reinvestment. For example, one due diligence officer ran several possible reinvestment schemes through the operating model and found that in all cases investor returns improved because of the reinvestment plans. But returns for the general partner also increased, and at a far faster rate because of the acquisition fees earned by the GP.

The only way to obtain a sense of the impact of various operating variables is to test the assumptions used in the model. In this case, this sponsor provided a copy of the model that was constructed on an IBM-compatible version of Lotus 1-2-3. Assumptions can also be further tested by using historical figures obtained from prior fund performance.

Equipment leasing involves depleting assets. Reinvestment is required to produce long-term gains and to overcome the impact of high front-end loads associated with all limited partnership investments. The only possible exception would be a full-payout program where there is some likelihood or residual value appreciation, as some aircraft leasing programs have promised. However, this is an unlikely scenario and still does not produce high enough returns to justify the high cost of initial program fees. The bottom line is that equipment leasing invloves depreciating assets. From an economic view, there is little room to generate long-term investor gains without some form of reinvestment program. The only other possible means of avoiding program reinvestment would be a dramatic change in existing tax law, where the tax consequences of possible write-offs would out-weigh the economic realities of leasing. This is unlikely.

After-Tax Projections

Figure 15.2 shows after-tax projections for this sample container leasing fund over the life of the program. In this base case, a combined federal and state investor tax rate of 33 percent was used. A six-year straight-line depreciable life was used for income tax purposes. A 6 percent per anum interest rate was used to calculate interest income on cash balances. Overall, the sponsor's projection shows an 11.5 percent net after-tax internal rate of return. (IRR is defined as the discount rate that causes the net present value of net future cash flow to equal zero.)

Many software programs are available to calculate investor after-tax yields. Our purpose is not to promote proprietary programs or to suggest yet one more model. What we do recommend is that financial advisors and investors compare the projected rates of return against competing investments, using different reinvestment rates. For example, Figure 15.3 shows a 7 percent reinvestment rate for the best case after-tax distributions from the container leasing fund based on an initial $10,000 investment with the investor in a 28 percent tax bracket. This investment is compared with a municipal bond invest-ment of $10,000 which pays $693 each year with the initial bond investment returned in 2001.

Figure 15.3 indicates an annual 11.6 percent after-tax IRR for the municipal bond investment compared to a 15.78 percent best case after-tax IRR for the container leasing fund. Of course, the financial advisor can change the reinvestment rates to suit his or her own expectations. What is important to the after-tax yield analysis of a leasing fund is that it be compared with alternative investments. In this illustration, the decision must be influenced by the level of comparative risk perceived by the individual investor. A four-point IRR advantage for the leasing fund over the municipal bond may be enough for the investor to overcome the perceived riskiness of the leasing investment. If, however, the base case for the container leasing fund was used with its 11.5 percent after-tax IRR, then the decision to invest may change.

Figure 15.3 also shows a shorter payback period for the leasing investment, in eight years versus eleven for the municipal bond. Still, we need to be aware that the cash distributions from an equipment leasing fund include a portion of capital. The depletion rate of the investor's capital contribution will depend on the nature of the equipment. Most computer peripheral equipment will fall to a negligible residual value in about five years. Thus, a computer leasing fund will have to generate more cash than another type of equipment whose residual value holds up longer.

For many investors, it may be a good strategy to plan on reinvesting a portion of annual cash distributions from the leasing fund to recoup the original investment. Figure 15.4 shows how an investor can reinvest a portion of current cash distributions to recoup the original investment. In this illustration, the leasing fund generates cash distributions of between 13 to 15 percent during the first six years of the 10-year program. In the last four years of the program, during which time the assets will be liquidated, cash returns are roughly 23 percent. Total projected cash returns for this hypothetical leasing fund would be $17,650.

The investor wants to ensure the return of his original $10,000 investment. In Figure 15.4, using an 8 percent reinvestment rate (compounded annually), the investor calculates the future value of his $10,000 original investment at the end of the 10-year program to be roughly $15,549. To recover the $10,000 originally invested, he must reinvest a portion of each year's cash distribution at 8 percent. In this case, the investor decides to reinvest roughly one-half of cash distributions during the first six years of the program. In the final four years of the program, the investor reinvests roughly two-thirds of cash distributions.

Without any reinvestment plan, the investor in this hypothetical leasing fund would obtain a total cash return of $17,650. With the reinvestment scheme, the investor spends $7,125 during the program and reinvests the remaining $10,525 at 8 percent which is worth $15,549 at the end of the program.

In Summary

What we've tried to illustrate in this chapter is that leasing fund yield analysis is really an assessment of the operating assumptions that underlie the financial projections. The key assumptions involve lease

Figure 15.3
**Comparison of 7% Municipal Bond with Investment in TCC
Equipment Income Fund
Assumption: $10,000 Investment, 28% Tax Rate**

AFTER TAX CASH FLOW

| | Municipal Bond | | TCC Equipment Income Fund | |
	Cash	Cumulative**	After-tax cash	Cumulative**
1988*	693	693	690	690
1989	693	1,434	1,200	1,938
1990	693	2,228	1,116	3,190
1991	693	3,077	1,157	4,570
1992	693	3,985	1,200	6,090
1993	693	4,957	1,257	7,773
1994	693	5,997	1,016	9,333
1995	693	7,110	2,017	12,003***
1996	693	8,301	1,970	14,813
1997	693	9,575	1,819	17,669
1998	693	10,938***	1,706	20,612
1999	693	12,938	1,668	23,723
2000	693	13,957	1,627	27,010
2001	$ 10,693	$25,627	$3,193	$32,094
Average After-tax return/Yr.:		11.16%		15.78%

*   Assumes Investment made in January, and 1% Commission for Bond Purchase.
**   Assumes Reinvestment Rate of 7%.
*** Payback

Source: Textainer Capital Corp.

rental rates, residual values, fund operating costs, and reinvestment strategies. These assumptions should be held up to the light of industry norms and prior performance of the fund manager.

Some of the operating assumptions have far greater impact than other variables, depending on how the fund is structured. In general terms, the longer the life of the program, the less impact is felt by residual values and front-load fees. The type of equipment under management affects residual assumptions and ultimate yields. A computer or other high-tech fund requires higher cash returns than another longer-life equipment such as transportation equipment. A fund reinvestment strategy is important to sustain the assets under management. Often, the individual investor may want to reinvest a portion of fund cash distributions to ensure this return of original investment.

Figure 15.4
Equipment Leasing Income Fund Annual Cash Distributions

| Year | Initial Capital | Cash Flow from Lease Investment | | | Reinvestment Amount @ 8% (Compounded Annually) | | Total Cash Reivced Overall |
		Annual Distribution	Amount Spent Annually	Amount Reinvested Annually	Compounding Period	Value at End of Period	
1	($10,000)	+ 1,300	- 600	= 700	10		
2		+ 1,300	- 625	= 675	9		
3		+ 1,400	- 650	= 750	8		
4		+ 1,400	- 675	= 725	7		
5		+ 1,500	- 700	= 800	6		
6		+ 1,500	- 725	= 775	5		
7		+ 2,300	- 750	= 1,500	4		
8		+ 2,300	- 775	= 1,525	3		
9		+ 2,300	- 800	= 1,500	2		
10		+ 2,350	- 825	= 1,525	1		
Total	(10,000)	$ 7,125				$15,549	$22,674

Source: Held Capital Companies

16

Evaluating the General Partner

All other factors are subordinate to the quality of the general partner when making the decision to invest in an equipment leasing fund.

No single factor—neither the fund's business plan nor investment objectives nor the market expectations of the equipment—can overcome the inadequacy of the fund's management. And as in any business enterprise, the true test of the management comes when something goes wrong. In leasing, this test is most crucial when the equipment comes back from the lessees.

We hope to present a number of ways in which the financial advisor and investor can get a better idea of the caliber of fund management before the decision to invest is made. Once the investment is made, the limited partner is unable to get out of the program easily. The time to cut losses is in the beginning of the investment decision-making process.

Leasing Fund Experience

It is usually an unwarranted risk to pick a public leasing fund that is managed by a first-time general partner. Even a first-time public fund sponsor should have demonstrated the ability to manage such a program through a prior history of successfully managing a number of private funds. How many funds has the general partner managed? How have they performed? Over what period of time? Have any gone full cycle, that is, have any programs been operated and liquidated as planned?

The ability to market a leasing program successfully to the

financial services industry is in itself not a demonstration of equipment leasing expertise. We say this because it has become an unfortunate experience of the limited partnership industry that many program syndicators have shown remarkable skills is raising money through the financial services distribution system but have not shown an equal skill in making money for limited partners who have invested in their financial products.

Because few equipment leasing income programs have gone full cycle, the financial advisor has a responsibility to his investing clients to do all that is possible to distinguish between the financial and fund operating track record of the program sponsor. This is especially true in the public leasing fund marketplace, because the rapid growth of leasing fund industry sales may have attracted a lot of me-too syndication firms which are simply riding a short-term trend and have not demonstrated an ability to manage complex leasing programs in all stages of the business cycle.

A review of the balance sheet of the general partner is also recommended. Does the general partner have deep pockets to weather uncertainties and short-term operating disruptions? Does the general partner have the financial capacity and staying power necessary to manage a leasing program for 7, 10, or 15 years?

Remarketing History

We said at the outset that a leasing fund general partner is best tested when the equipment comes off lease. The success of most leasing income funds is largely determined through the remarketing of equipment and ongoing lease management. The ability to keep equipment on lease or release equipment many times over to new lessees and the ability to acquire and dispose of equipment effectively is crucial to any fund, but essential when leasing equipment such as computers or other high-tech equipment where the residual bet is so significant to the fund's ultimate return to investors.

The obvious way to check out the ability of the general partner to remarket equipment is to review the leasing history of equipment that has been managed over the years. Some of the key indicators include equipment utilization, percentage of equipment off-lease, lessee default rates, record of residuals obtained on the full range of equipment to be managed, lease rates, and secondary release rates. Every operating claim included in the sponsor's investor projections should be backed up with a solid history of leasing and managing the equipment. If, for example, the general partner is projecting lease rentals far in excess of prior history what assurance does the potential investor have that these numbers are not just wishful thinking?

Key Indicators of Equipment Lease Management

Percent Equipment Off-Lease. A general partner needs to maintain at least 90 percent of the partnership's equipment assets on lease at all times. While this is a crude rule of thumb, and relates primarily to operating types of leases, it does recognize informal standards among leasing operators. This percentage will vary with changes in the economic climate and is subject to some interpretation, but it remains essential that the general partner demonstrate a long-term ability to maintain equipment on lease—in goods times and bad. Another way to measure idle assets is the weighted average of time that the equipment remains unleased. This will often indicate specific types of equipment in the portfolio that are problems.

Percent Lessee Defaults. Most leasing operators look for a default rate of less than 2 percent among their client lessees. This is an overall figure and can vary depending on whether the equipment is under full-payout or operating lease. Abrupt surges in the level of defaults from one year to the next may indicate an inability to manage credit risks.

Lease Rental Rates. Initial lease rate factors (based on the net monthly rental income as a percentage of equipment cost) should meet or exceed the equipment norms listed in Figures 6.1 and 8.1 for computer equipment. Secondary release rates can vary widely, but generally a leasing operator needs to demonstrate a healthy renewal percentage. For example, what percentage of lessees renew lease of the equipment? A rough gauge of operating leases is that more than half of the equipment is renewed by the original lessee. Secondary and tertiary lease rates should not show a dramatic falloff in rental income. Release rates need to be compared to residual value estimates. If, for example, equipment is expected to lose one-third of its value in two years, then the release rate of the equipment after two years should not be lower than one-third of the original lease rate.

Residual Values.   The adequacy of residual values obtained by the leasing operator is demonstrated by the release or sale of the equipment. Figures 6.1 and 8.1 also provide indicators of the level of residual values for different types of equipment.

A growing trend among some leasing fund syndicators is to operate the program with a co-general partner whose experience is in equipment leasing management. Under such a setup, the co-general partners are supposed to do what they do best. In effect, the financially experienced co-general partner acts as the asset manager who should supervise the ongoing leasing activities of the equipment-oriented co partner. This arrangement can make sense to the investor but it also means the fund syndicator must accept lower revenues. For the latter reason, many syndicators opt to do it all themselves, even if their skills lie elsewhere.

You cannot acquire equipment leasing experience overnight, and this should be a warning sign to financial advisors. The advisor or investor needs to be assured of the skill of the principals managing the fund. The prospectus will list the senior managers of the leasing fund, and this can provide some idea of management experience. It is important to look for stability of management. Very often, the top and mid-level management of the fund has only been in place a short time. Some sponsors tout a long history of accomplishment, but sometimes the managers who made that money in prior programs have left the general partner's employ. The principals of the general partner should be experienced in the specific equipment to be managed and should have the staff support to do the job properly.

It is a good idea to find out how many people and systems the general partner uses to support the leasing operation. Experienced leasing staff costs money. Backroom support is an area where some general partners cut back. For example, how prompt and efficient is the general partner in servicing limited partners? Are investor communications and financial statements handled effectively. Administering the financial statements of a public limited partnership requires substantial accounting, legal, and administrative support. Is that support there?

The best way to tell if there is substantial accounting, legal, and administrative support is through the due diligence visits to the sponsor's offices. How are past programs administered? What expertise and support staff does the sponsor have? What computer systems does the sponsor have to ensure timely investor reports for tax purposes? How well are the records and accounts of the partnerships managed? Many of the answers to these questions will also come from contacts with broker/dealers and other investors who have done business with the sponsor in prior programs. An investigation of how well the sponsor has serviced limited partners in the past is essential in determining whether the general partner has the resources to adequately serve investor needs. As for legal opinions, the sponsor's prospectus should provide clear opinions on questions of tax liability in the offering statement. We describe some of these issues in greater detail in chapters 19 and 20.

Identity of Interest with Investors

The general partner can demonstrate identity of interest with limited partners in a number of ways, few of which are commonplace. A good place to start is if the general partner puts some of his own money into the program. Very often, the general partner will put up only a token amount of money to get a public program started. In a privately offered limited partnership, it is almost a requirement that the general partner put a significant amount of his or her own money to demonstrate faith in the investment.

Another persuasive means of showing identity of interest with limited partners is to defer management fees and incentives until later stages of the leasing program. If so much of the overall return to investors is dependent on the successful management of the later stages of the program, then is it too much to ask the general partner to wait along with the investors for the bulk of GP compensation?

Some fund general partners start sharing immediately in cash distributions, as much as 10 to 15 percent of regular investor distributions over and above other management fees and incentives. For no capital contribution, or a token one at best, some general partners will begin taking a percentage of cash distributions. And what relative share of investor distributions does the general partner assume during all stages of the program—acquisition, reinvestment, operating and liquidation phases?

A further indication of the general partner's willingness to identify with investor concerns can show up in legal proceedings that may be active against the sponsor. Sometimes these legal actions may involve disgruntled investors or former employees and may be revealed in the offering prospectus. These reports of lawsuits make interesting reading in a prospectus. If a sponsor has a pattern of walking away from some prior partnerships, that may show up in such lawsuits.

The quality of the sponsor's due diligence information is a good indication of identity with investor interests. Due diligence, as everyone in the financial services industry knows, far too often can become just a phrase included in U.S. securities law. The average financial advisor or planner has little time to perform a good due diligence investigation of a leasing fund. Even due diligence officers for broker/dealers have a limited amount of time to report on the appropriateness of an investment, and often, many of these due diligence officers have limited experience with equipment leasing funds. The leasing fund general partner can improve the standing of his own offering with sales and due diligence information that really seeks to inform and answer advisor's questions. A fund sponsor's financial information package should be specific, substantive, and short on hyperbole.

Industry Recommendations

The lease operating record of the general partner can be understood better by those also in the industry. Some of the best ways to learn more about an equipment leasing operator is to ask those who compete with the sponsor. Some of this work is more logically left to the due diligence officer, but a phone call or two could help the financial advisor get a feel for the sponsor's standing in the business. If, for example, the general partner makes a claim about an industry or type of equipment market, and it does not sound factual, a trade publication or a competitor in the industry can be consulted to see if the claim is substantiated.

A person is also judged by the company he or she keeps, and the same goes for a general partner. Checking with registered broker/dealers who have approved the fund is always a good idea. While a financial advisor or planner is often affiliated with a particular registered securities dealer, it is also recommended that a financial advisor speak to other professionals who have purchased the sponsor's financial products in the past.

The most obvious way to review the management of a leasing program is to compare the fund and its management against other competing funds currently being offered. Several financial industry publications, such as the *Stanger Report, Financial Planning* magazine, and others, publish summaries of leasing fund offerings and even rank offering terms of public partnerships (see Appendix C for a listing of financial publications and equipment leasing information resources).

When Things Go Wrong

The true test of management is when events go awry. The economy usually goes sour every few years. Any established equipment leasing operator should be able to demonstrate a steady performance under less-than-ideal circumstances. A long history in business is usually one way to indicate management ability. A good plan can help, but people make money and people execute plans drafted by other people. Sometimes there is no guide. We recommend that financial advisors ask "what-if" questions about management abilities, as well as in plugging financial variables in the computer model of the program. What if a major equipment supplier files for bankruptcy, what will the general partner do? What does the lessor do when the equipment comes back on a default? What if projected lease rentals are not what the sponsor anticipated, what will the general partner do to meet investor objectives?

Handling Possible Conflicts

The general partner usually manages equipment leasing activities for his own account or for corporate affiliates and prior partnerships. Conflicts can arise in any number of ways between what might be best for your partnership and others that may be managed by the general partner. How are leases and equipment allocated between the various partnerships or affiliates? How does the potential investor know his fund will not get the worst leases, or no leases, at the expense of other affiliates?

An equipment leasing general partner can forestall some of these issues by specifying or even guaranteeing how fund assets may be handled in gray areas of possible conflicts of interest. A leasing fund sponsor should indicate to potential investors in advance what criteria will be used in the acquisition, lease, and disposition of equipment for the fund and other funds managed by the general partner.

17

Offering Terms and Management Fees

Analysis of the impact of offering terms on equipment leasing partnerships shows that these fees can affect the investor's after-tax returns by as much as 30 percent over the life of the program. The impact of these management and offering fees—regardless of the partnership's actual performance—is reason enough for financial advisors to carefully compare the differences among competing investments. In some cases, certain fee provisions may even demonstrate a lack of real concern for investor interests.

How are leasing partnership fees structured? For the most part, leasing partnership syndicators follow guidelines established by the North American Securities Administrators Association (NASAA). But there can be a great deal of variance among sponsor offering terms. We want to look at how these fees are structured and how they can be compared to similar leasing programs.

Fee Stages

General partner and syndication fees are divided into three primary categories which correspond to the three stages of the partnership's life cycle. The first group of fees are front-end costs which include offering, organizational, and equipment acquisition fees. NASAA guidelines suggest the limitation of front-end fees to a maximum of 20 percent of limited partners' investment on an unleveraged program. This front-end percentage fee can go up to 25 percent in programs that use debt. The maximum 25 percent front-end load for a leveraged fund would be permitted in a fund with up to 80 percent debt. The reasoning is that the extra debt involves additional equipment acquisition which justifies the additional cost as a percentage of the original investment by the limited partner.

Management compensation during the operational stages of the leasing program depends on the kind of leases that the general partner is writing. Full-payout leases permit up to 2 percent in management fees as a percentage of leasing revenues. An operating lease permits up to 5 percent in management fees as a percentage of revenues. In some instances where the general partner assumes a direct role in the remarketing of operating leases, management operational fees can go as high as 7 percent of leasing revenues. The rationale here is that operating leases require more management expertise and energy because the general partner must release, renew, or remarket the equipment as contrasted with the typical full-payout lease where lease expenses and profits are covered by cash revenues over the lease term.

The general partner is also permitted reasonable incentive fees during the operational stage of the partnership. NASAA guidelines permit the general partner to take another 5 percent of cash distributions until the investor recoups his capital contribution plus a cumulative adjusted return of 8 percent. Once this investor objective has been met, the general partner is permitted 15 percent of all subsequent cash distributions.

Of keen interest to the financial advisor and investor is the willingness of the general partner to adjust the management share of incentive fees so that less is taken during the early stages of the program for a higher percentage in the later stage. Because the bulk of most leasing program returns are contingent on the later stages of the fund, an incentive fee structure that is subordinate to the long-term goals of the investor helps demonstrate identity of interest with limited partner concerns.

During the liquidation stage of the program when the equipment is to be disposed, NASAA guidelines suggest that the general partner can take up to 3 percent of cash proceeds on the sale of the equipment as compensation.

However, NASAA fee guidelines are only suggestions. And while the great majority of public partnership sponsors work within the fee guidelines, there is substantial variation, particularly within the operational phase of the program.

Front-end fees are also a significant factor in all limited partnership calculations. Here is a typical case of where the front-end fees go in a leasing program:

Type of Fee	Percent of Investor Capital
Organizational expense	3%
Wholesaling costs	2
Selling costs	8
Equipment acquisition	3
Debt placement costs (when used)	0.5
Due diligence	0.5
Total front load	17%

Figure 17.1 shows the results of a survey of equipment leasing public program offering terms. As you can see, the range of fee variation among the highest- and lowest-rated programs is substantial. Among the 20 leasing funds that were surveyed, the lowest front-end fees were 9.8 percent of investors' original contribution compared to the highest program front end fees which were 27 percent, above the maximum guidelines from NASAA. Average front-end fees were 16.5 percent in this leasing fund survey.

The variation in operational fees was even more substantial. Full-payout lease management fees ranged from 1.5 percent of lease revenues to a high of 6 percent—four times as great. The general partner's unsubordinated share of cash distribution also showed substantial differences from program to program, from 0 to 10 percent for the lowest- and highest-ranked fee structures.

Bottom Line Impact

Using a statistical sensitivity model to compare offering terms among public leasing programs, the *Stanger Report* of Shrewsbury, Connecticut, reported several major findings in its survey:

- The internal rate of return can be affected by as much as 30

Figure 17.1
Offering Terms in Equipment Leasing Funds

	Average Fees	Lowest Fees	Highest Fees
Front-End Fees:			
Brokerage Commissions	9.0%	7.0%	10.5%
Organizational & Offering Costs	3.0	1.3	6.5
Acquisition Fees & Expenses[1]	4.5	1.5	10.0
Operational Phase Fees:			
Equipment Management Fees[2]:			
Full-Payout Leases	2.8%	1.5%	6.0%
Operating Leases	5.2	3.5	7.0
GP Unsubordinated Share	4.4	0.0	10.0
GP Subordinated Share	9.6	0.0	14.6
Subordination (Annual Return to LP)	ROC* + 8.6	—	ROC* + 8.0
Liquidation Phase Fees:			
GP Unsubordinated Share	2.7%	1.0%	10.0%
GP Subordinated Share	12.2	0.0	18.6
Subordination of GP Share	ROC* + 8.6	—	ROC* + 9.0
Sales Commissions	2.6	0.0	3.5
Subordination of Sales Commission	ROC* + 7.6	—	0.0
Stanger's Offering Terms Ranking	AA+ (65.7)	AAA+ (77.2)	A (54.3)

* Return of Capital.
[1] Expressed as a percentage of equipment purchase price.
[2] Expressed as a percentage of gross revenues.

Note: Line entries show the average, lowest and highest fee in the fee category indicated. Therefore, the "least favorable" and "most favorable" columns do not represent composite fees in any individual program.

Source: Stanger Report, October 1987.

percent by offering terms alone—from 10.20 to 12.95 percent.

- The leasing program most expensive to the limited partner investor would need to sustain up to 50 percent more residual value of the equipment to equal the same rate of return as the least expensive program.

- The most significant impact on overall investor returns is from operational fees, followed by front-end fees. Liquidation fees have the smallest impact on investor returns and diminish as residual values decline. This is all the more significant to financial advisors and investors because the typical equipment leasing program will bet heavily on the residual value of the equipment under management.

Judging Management Fees

Not all leasing sponsors have equal experience, and this, some general partners argue, justifies higher average fees for their program.

The *Stanger Report* publishes offering term rankings for equipment leasing (as well as for real estate, cable TV, and oil and gas partnerships) which can provide some guidance on fees. Using a computer sensitivity model, Stanger will rank competing partnerships from BBB to AAA+, with a total of seven-ranked classifications. In effect, the model compares an investment in a public leasing partnership with an equal amount in a direct leasing (unloaded) investment. An important consideration of the Stanger ranking is that it uses only offering terms and program projections provided by the sponsor. The ranking does not include historical sponsor performance. In other words, the model does not compare historical performance among the fee structures of competing programs. Another question is that the Stanger ranking can be adjusted before the ranking is published, if the sponsor uses the rating service for a consulting fee and makes suggested changes in the program's offering terms. In addition, not all fee areas are covered by the Stanger model, which means that a sponsor may conceivably improve its rating by shifting fees into areas uncovered by the model. However, the Stanger ranking does separate its analysis by type of equipment managed, creating five different classes for aircraft, other transportation equipment (rail cars, marine containers, tractor/trailers), computers, medical equipment, and manufacturing equipment. This permits a direct comparison of different leasing program structures.

The independent ranking of offering terms provides some indication of relative general partner fees. Due diligence officers for broker/dealers should also evaluate offering terms for reasonableness before the program is approved for sale by the dealer's representatives and planners. Broker/dealer due diligence can approach 2 percent of the investors' contribution, and it is reasonable to ask the securities dealer's due diligence people to carefully evaluate general partner fees (see chapter 20).

In some instances fee percentages can be deceiving. This occurs when certain fixed types of costs are absorbed in larger program offerings. For example, it is not logical that fee percentages for legal, printing, and other organizational costs should be the same in a $100 million partnership offering as they would be in a much smaller program of say, $10 million. It does not cost 10 times as much to print the same number of prospectuses in the larger program.

Worst Cases

In some rare cases, a sponsor may include a fee that is hard to justify under any circumstance. An example reflects an instance where a general partner included a fee provision where in the event of a lessee default, the general partner was able to capture for his own account all of the lease commitment fee that had been deposited in escrow by the defaulting lessee. Sometimes these lease commitment fees can amount to 50 percent or more of the cost of the equipment. In effect, the general partner obtains this fee despite his own negligence in keeping the equipment on lease. The investor is out of the picture to the advantage of the general partner. This is an isolated case, but it does illustrate why fee structures should be carefully reviewed.

A basic warning sign for a financial advisor is whenever the general partner exceeds the recommended fees by the North American Securities Administrators Association. If a general partner is managing relatively low risk full-payout types of leases, there is little or no justification to exceed the operational fee guideline of 2 percent of lease revenues by imposing a 6 percent fee as was cited earlier in a survey of leasing partnerships.

Subordination

The best guide for financial advisors is to look for general partner subordination of operating stage fees to later phases of the program's management. Which is preferable?—when the general partner postpones general partner cash distribution to the full return of investors' original investment or when the general partner takes 10 percent of cash distributions (on top of 5 percent operating fees) right from the start of the operation?

Liquidation sales fees should also be subordinated to the investors' return of capital plus a target cumulative rate of return. If, for example, the general partner decides to liquidate the program earlier than anticipated, doesn't it make sense to the investor that the full return of original capital precede the liquidation sales commission fees? This would also be the recommendation if the general partner was engaged in an aggressive reinvestment program during the life of the program. In this case, the investor would prefer to have the general partner lower or defer some of the acquisition fees on reinvestment to the return of investor capital.

18
Danger Signs

There are a variety of danger signs that financial advisors can spot in an equipment leasing partnership offering. The trick is knowing what to look for. This chapter suggests specific areas where potential downside trouble can be found and avoided during the program review process.

Who's in Charge?

The first order of business is in judging the character and capacity of the general partner who will manage the investors' money over the 5 to 14 year life of the typical program. There is a danger in picking a public fund that is to be managed by a general partner with less than five years experience in managing leasing partnerships or leasing experience with the specific equipment to be acquired by the fund. But this is not a failsafe criterion.

A general partner may have developed any number of leasing funds but have failed to produce for investors. One way to check on the value of prior funds managed by the general partner, aside from fund balance sheets which can be misleading, is to see if any of those funds are being traded on secondary markets for limited partnerships. A number of securities dealers make a market in different limited partnerships, including leasing funds, and this may be a source of independent market data on the value of the sponsor's prior funds.

If the sponsor's prior funds are not traded on a secondary market, why not? Such a lack of a market for the sponsor's earlier funds may indicate trouble or just that the sponsor has not yet demonstrated a record of performance. If one or more of the sponsor's earlier funds are traded, how does the secondary market offering price compare to the book value of limited partner shares and the original leasing partnership investment? If the secondary fund units are trading far below book value, then there likely is a lack of faith in the fund and by association, a corresponding lack of faith in the general partner.

Conversely, if a general partner's prior fund units are selling above book value and reasonably close to the original limited partner investment, the secondary marketplace is effectively affirming the value of the fund and the general partner. This kind of response on secondary markets, along with the history of prior fund cash distributions will provide the financial advisor and investor with a more informed expectation for the current leasing fund under investment consideration.

The lack of deep pockets on the part of the general partner is also a danger sign. If the general partner is undercapitalized to properly handle his fiduciary duties for the partnership, then investors should stop and avoid assuming the role of banker for this fund manager.

Abrupt Cash Drops

If the general partner has a history of managing leasing funds, quarterly and annual financial reports will be available for inspection, in the offering prospectus, through due diligence materials and in 10Q quarterly and 10K annual filings with the Securities and Exchange Commission. A telltale sign of problems is any abrupt drop in lease rental income.

Sometimes, especially in the first two to three years of the program's operation, a sponsor may be distributing projected cash to the limited partners but at the expense of partnership assets, and not because the cash has been earned from the actual operation. What can happen is that a sponsor will continue to make these cash distributions to avoid embarrassment, and not because the money has been earned in the operation of the fund.

There have been instances where a sponsor will continue to distribute cash, even though unearned, to keep other syndication activities going. This tactic can not be kept up for long but it can be spotted when reviewing recent financial data. If, for example, the sponsor is paying 12 to 15 percent annual cash distributions to the lease parnters, but the fund's operation indicates an abrupt drop in lease rentals or just a below-par performance on partnership assets from prior funds, then something's out of kilter. If the sponsor is busily raising money on a number of other partnerships in syndication, and not showing actual results in the operation of prior funds, then the danger is even more palpable to the prospective investor.

We recommend that prior programs be investigated to judge if the sponsor is distributing more cash than warranted by the earning performance of the fund. What is the cash distribution as a percentage of investor assets? What is the percentage of fund cash flow per investor assets? By reviewing past program balance sheets and income statements, the investor and financial advisor can gauge if the sponsor is sacrificing fund assets. In effect, is the sponsor diluting long-term limited partner interests by liquidating asset values? Or, more troubling, is the sponsor covering up actual lease earnings weakness and—in effect—creating something of a Ponzi-scheme where ultimately the structure will collapse because there are neither earnings nor asset growth to support future returns to the investors?

Conflicts of Interest

We've mentioned the potential for general partner conflicts of interest through joint ventures between the partnership and other affiliates or entities controlled by the general partner. One way to probe more deeply into this possibility is to review the performance of the general partner as compared to the performance of partnerships managed by the general partner.

The first step is to see how all the partnerships managed by the general partners compare. Are some weaklings and others high flyers? This *may* indicate that the general partner is managing some of the funds for maximum cash flow at the expense of other funds. The problem is that transactions among the partnerships and affiliates controlled by the general partners are not arms-length transactions. The limited partners do not vote on these joint ventures. Almost always the leasing partnership does not know the details of these transactions.

The second step is to compare the performance of the general partner's funds against the performance of the general partners. If some, all, or most of these funds are distributing less than expected cash to the investors, how does this compare to the general partner's own earnings from operations? If the general partner's own earnings are well above the fund's performance, the financial advisor has to wonder if this has been achieved at the expense of the limited partners.

Conflicts in operating the funds can occur in any number of ways. Selling equipment from one fund to another at inflated prices is one possibility. Remember, the general partner is being paid a commission on the sale of the equipment by both the seller (Fund A) and by the buyer (Fund B) and the temptation to earn commissions can override the interests of the limited partners.

One way to assure investors in advance is to establish guarantees and guidelines at the start that will limit this potential for conflicts of interest. If, for example, equipment to be acquired is specified before the fund starts operation, the financial advisor can look to see if any of the general partner's affiliates or other funds are the owners of the equipment. Independent appraisals of this equipment should be obtained and presented to the potential investors and financial advisors to justify the proposed sale price.

Litigation

We have a great deal of litigation in the United States, and a lawsuit filed against a general partner is, in itself, no indication of misfeasance or malfeasance. However, the facts or claims in the litigation may indicate danger signals to the advisor and investor. Are there employee lawsuits by former executives of the general partner? Does the lawsuit portend a serious issue of future management of the proposed fund? We've mentioned before that leasing management is a specialized type of experience that is not transferable from other industries. The walkout of former executives is a sign of discontinuity of general partner management. It should not be ignored.

Sometimes pending litigation will indicate a lack of adequate management when the going gets tough. One case happened when a corporate lessee of several business aircraft managed by the general partner defaulted on the lease of the equipment. The equipment had been 50 percent leveraged, and the debt was held by a major banking institution. The bank got nervous about the default and on its own ordered the aircraft to be sold at a distress price, against the urging of the general partner. The bank was only concerned about its 50 percent loan on the equipment. The bank was a secured creditor and, even at the distress price, was able to get its money back. Not so for the limited partners, who took a bath because of the default and hastiness of the lender. Just bad luck? Maybe, but the general partner should have taken greater steps to prevent this action by the bank, either through better negotiation of the loan covenant, or just by reducing the partnership's debt exposure.

Limited partner lawsuits may also indicate a lack of character and capacity in the general partner. One limited partner lawsuit or even a couple over a long period of general partner management does not necessarily show any lack of character, but a pattern of limited partner lawsuits might do just that. The offering prospectus and the audited financial statements of the general partner will briefly indicate the status of litigation for or against the general partner, and we recommend reviewing this material with care.

Uninvested Cash

There is always a delay in the investment of investor proceeds with the start-up of a new fund. Depending on the nature of the equipment and if there is a specified list of potential lease activity in advance, the period of initial fund investment can reasonably take as much as one year after the fund has closed for sale or been fully subscribed.

However, some funds will go for several years with substantial sums of investor cash uninvested in the proposed equipment. One venture leasing fund had gone for almost three years and still had almost one-half of the limited partner's investment sitting in cash accounts. This is an extreme example, but a quick review of prior fund balance sheets will indicate how effectively the general partner is investing in the proposed equipment.

Less easy to spot is the case when equipment sits idle—unleased and unsold—for lengthy periods of time. The only way to determine this is for the financial professional, usually the due diligence officer, to review and audit individual pieces of equipment in the general partner's managed portfolio of prior funds. If a pattern is apparent, something is lacking in the capacity of the general partner. Naturally, this might be the result of several factors, but none of the possible factors indicates skilled fund management.

Unbalanced Investment

The leasing fund investor needs to be assured that his capital is being protected against unusual risks of overinvestment in one equipment vendor or in a single type of equipment. Specified equipment and lessees can satisfy this need. Another way is for the general partner to set specific limits on investing in any single vendor or type of equipment.

If a general partner has more than 30 percent in any single vendor, then the financial advisor should be concerned. Many computer funds, for example, put most or all of the equipment into IBM equipment. This may sound risk-free, but it is not. There is nothing to prevent IBM from changing its pricing and marketing strategy or introducing a new product which could seriously affect the value of the earlier IBM equipment. We should also be aware that IBM has continued to lose market share in significant segments of the computer industry, and merely putting the label of IBM on the equipment does not assure success; the failure of IBM's PC Jr being one case in point.

Blind Pools

Most leasing funds are investments in blind pools of equipment. Still, this fact does not give the potential investor any security about how his money will be invested. All things being equal, an investment in a specified pool of equipment is to be preferred by the financial advisor over the blind pool. This is only common sense.

If a general partner avoids specifying leases or types of equipment to be acquired, then he adds an extra element of uncertainty to the investment. Sometimes the general partner can confuse the situation by stating in the offering materials that he may purchase a tremendous variety of equipment, from personal computers to airplanes, from medical to manufacturing equipment. But this really says little. The potential investor wants to know with some certainty what the general partner will acquire, not what he might acquire for the fund.

Fees Exceed NASAA Guidelines

We see no reason for a general partner to charge management or incentive fees in excess of guidelines established by the partnership industry's organization, the North American Securities Administrators Association. There is ample flexibility there already.

Overselling

All too frequently, leasing funds have been sold to the wrong people for the wrong reasons. Because leasing income partnerships are fixed investments, some sales representatives compare them to other competing fixed investments, such as government-backed securities or AAA-rated corporate bonds. This is inappropriate.

Leasing partnerships, as all limited partnerships, provide no assurance that the original investment will be returned in whole. Because leasing funds involve investment in equipment whose value depletes significantly during the life of the partnership, there can be no guarantees of future value of the equipment many years out.

The danger to avoid is the overselling of leasing funds in the first place. There is a significant risk of operating the fund and managing the assets. These risks are not trivial, and this is why investor returns must exceed other, more secure investments in competing fixed-income investments such as government securities or highly rated corporate bonds. We say this is a danger, because many knowledgeable sources in the leasing funds business are well aware that funds were unfortunately sold on this basis. In effect, the real nature of the risk and the economics were not presented fully to the investor or even the financial advisor and planner. This is one reason why leasing income funds should form a smaller portion of an investor's portfolio and should be balanced by other investments that diversify risks to optimize the objectives of the investor.

Along this line, the author has developed a very subjective bias in evaluating partnership sales materials. If the selling brochures and promotional material include an abundance of glossy, four-color pictures and splashy graphics, without a corresponding detail of fund assumptions and objectives, then this offering has raised a caution light. Admittedly, this is a highly intuitive decision, but it tends to be more right than wrong after all is said and done, and unfortunately, in these flashy sales materials, more is often said than done.

Rollups and MLPs

Few, if any, master limited partnerships are being used in equipment leasing funds. They have become a target of the Internal Revenue Service and will not be attractive to investors if these entities are subject to corporate taxation. Such taxation would defeat the entire purpose of partnerships to pass through benefits to limited partners. But there is another problem.

Limited partnerships are fixed investments. Efforts to create instant liquidity, such as through the device of an master limited partnership, distort how these funds are managed in the first place. Leasing funds must be managed for the long-term benefit of the investor. There is a clear life-cycle to these funds where assets must be used, managed, and disposed properly for investors to gain the anticipated benefit of the investment. To add liquidity, aside from IRS concerns, creates a short term emphasis which does not fit the management of the assets nor the long-term prospects of the fund.

During the brief spate of master limited partnership activity in 1986 and 1987, at least one major equipment leasing sponsor choose to rollup a number of prior leasing funds into one master limited partnership which was to be traded on a major stock exchange. This was done but at a significant dilution of the holdings of the prior partnership unit holders. The move permitted the sponsor to sell his syndication affiliate for a substantial premium. In effect, the limited partners of those prior funds were persuaded to buy the syndication affiliate which had the effect of diluting their investment in the equipment itself. It remains to be seen if such rollup activity is of any long term benefit to the investors involved. We think a sponsor with a history of rolling up prior partnerships into an master limited partnership, along with syndicating new, and competing partnerships, has a lot of explaining to do. It is a danger sign that should be investigated very carefully by financial professionals. Such arrangements by the fund sponsor do not strengthen the belief that he is an able manager of the equipment.

19
How to Read the Prospectus

The prospectus of a limited partnership offering is not designed for easy reading. The format of the prospectus is designed to meet legal and regulatory requirements. But it still includes the binding offer of the general partner to potential investors and covers all basic elements of the fund, except for financial projections which are prohibited from the prospectus by Securities and Exchange Commission rules.

The fact that financial projections are excluded from the offering prospectus is a mixed blessing for investors. On the one hand, investors are spared the excesses of promotional and speculative information in the basic offering statement. But investors and financial advisors must also seek other means to pin down sponsor assertions and assumptions about the operation of the fund.

The prospectus can be a useful means to make a quick initial review of the potential leasing partnership investment. Later, if the fund passes first muster and subsequent analysis and due diligence, the prospectus will become the document that spells out the obligations of the general partner to the limited partners.

Because the prospectus makes such dull reading over nearly 200 pages of text and charts, the financial advisor or investor may be tempted to rely too heavily on other sales-oriented materials from the sponsor. We will recommend a step-by-step method in this chapter to quickly review the key elements of the program that are included in the prospectus.

Figure 19.1 provides a worksheet that financial advisors can use to rank the basic elements of the partnership offering. The best use of the worksheet would be to review perhaps three or four competing leasing partnerships. The objective for the financial advisor would be to subjectively rank the program elements of several funds to obtain an initial level of interest in the competing offerings. The worksheet should be used only for similar types of partnerships, all equipment leasing, or all real estate, etc.

If the raw score is less than 20, or half the maximum possible initial ranking by the advisor, we suggest that the prospectus might be placed in a circular file. If one or more leasing funds are ranked higher than a total of 20, then there is a preference that should be further explored for detailed analysis and decision-making. The screening method is just a first phase in the evaluation process, but it will save the advisor a great deal of time and energy on programs that simply cannot make the first cut.

First Step: Investment Objectives

The prospectus is not intended to be read from cover to cover, starting from the beginning and proceeding through to the end as if you were reading a good novel. Use the table of contents on the back cover of the prospectus to quickly locate the important sections.

The first place to start is with the summary of the partnership and the offering, usually within the first few pages of the prospectus. A quick scan may indicate that the fund is not for you. More likely, the financial advisor will want to skip to the descriptions of key passages that give some specifics about the fund and its operation.

Investment objectives and policies (or sometimes called partnership business and policies,) should spell out in some detail the aims and strategy of the partnership. The more specific the objectives and policy, so much the better. The financial advisor should look for specific objectives, such as precise targets for cash distributions to investors, reinvestment policies, leverage to be used and equipment specification. What exactly will the general partner do to preserve investor capital? To what extent will limited partner returns be preferred over management fees? Under what conditions, if any, will debt be used in the fund? How much?

If this key section is overwhelmed by generalities instead of specifics, then the financial advisor may want to stop right there. A fuzzy description of investment objectives can hint at a program that is either not well planned or is trying to be all things to all people.

Figure 19.1
Initial Ranking of Equipment Leasing Partnership

Fund Name:
General Partner:
Broker/Dealer Approved:
Financial Advisor:

Ranking Date:

Prospectus Elements	Ranking Scale						Totals
	low 0	1	2	3	4	high 5	
Investment Objectives	0	1	2	3	4	5	
Managment	0	1	2	3	4	5	
Prior Performance/ Financials	0	1	2	3	4	5	
Risk Factors	0	1	2	3	4	5	
Compensation/Use of Proceeds	0	1	2	3	4	5	
Distribution Plan	0	1	2	3	4	5	
Conflicts of Interest	0	1	2	3	4	5	
Legal Matters/ Tax Consequences	0	1	2	3	4	5	

Total Ranked Score

Note: Score of less than 20 indicates lack of confidence in inital review of offering.

Step 2: Management

Who is running the show? What are their names and experiences? What is the history of the general partner? What are the responsibilities of the general partner? How are decisions made? For instance, who makes the decisions on equipment acquisition? Lessee credit? How are those decisions made?

Most of the guidelines given in chapter 16 will apply to reviewing the pedigree of the general partner and the key staff and executives. Biographies of the key players working for the general partner should indicate specific experience and qualifications to manage the assets of the partnership. We also suggest that the advisor look for turnover among the key players. A revolving door among the executive team is not a good sign.

Step 3: Prior Performance and Financials

Prior performance tables should include detailed financial information on the operation of prior public and in some cases, private programs sponsored and managed by the general partner. If the general partner has any history in the leasing funds business, the details should be included under several categories. Here are examples of schedules that would be included:

- Summary schedule of prior funds, including offering and use of investor proceeds, value of equipment purchased, effective lease rate factors for the fund, average lease terms, book value of equipment off-lease, and other operating data for each prior fund managed

- Schedule of prior equipment categories, including types, percentage of assets managed, purchase prices, residual values, and lease rate factors for each fund managed

- Schedule of how investor proceeds were applied in each fund

- Schedule of annual operating results for each fund managed

- Schedule of compensation paid to the general partner for each of the funds managed in prior years

In addition, the general partner should provide his own balance sheet and profit and loss statements to assess the general partner's own financial condition.

The financial advisor should be careful about interpreting the financial data from prior funds that were structured primarily as tax shelters. Only direct comparisons of income funds should be attempted in this initial review. What the advisor should be looking for in the review of prior performance is a pattern of success of cash distributions and operating results that give credence to the claims and projections that might be made for the fund.

Step 4: Risk Factors

As are described in chapter 5, a number of risk factors are inherent in any equipment leasing partnership, including the risk of operating leases, credit risks, risks associated with equipment residuals, debt, and other general business risks. Most often these risks are cited in general terms in the prospectus. However, the advisor should also be looking for more details about residual risks in this section or in another that may be devoted to the equipment under management. Very often, a leasing fund sponsor will provide independent appraisals of expected equipment residual values. If these residual values are specified, the financial advisor will have a basis for quickly evaluating the reasonableness of the estimates.

Step 5: Compensation/Use of Proceeds

The prospectus will usually describe general partner fees together with the estimated use of investor proceeds. The primary guide for the advisor is that these fee schedules are within partnership industry standards (chapter 17) and that the general partner subordinate his own incentives to the return of the investors' return of capital. The important areas for financial advisor concern are front-load costs and operational stage fees. Front-loads should not exceed 20 percent of total original investment and should be in line with other competing funds. At best, the general partner should delay his share of cash distributions until the investor has received all of his original investment back.

Step 6: Distribution Plan

This section of the prospectus will specify how the funds obtained through the offering will be handled and how sales commissions for qualified National Association of Securities Dealers representatives will be paid by the managing sales agent for the public offering. Details on minimum amounts of fund subscription and escrow arrangements will be described.

Step 7: Conflicts of Interest

In this section, the financial advisor is primarily looking for some form of guarantee from the general partner to assure the investor what steps the general partner will take to prevent possible conflicts of interest. These assurances may include percentage limits on acquisition, lease, disposition, and allocation of costs between the fund offering and other funds or equipment that may be managed by the general partner.

Step 8: Legal Matters/Tax Consequences

This section will include expert legal and tax opinion of the assertions presented in the offering statement. Outstanding litigation may provide clues to the character and capacity of the general partner. Details on the opinion of tax experts will also be presented which can assist the advisor in judging the tax implications of the fund for his client's investment. Because of the change in tax laws, the issue of passive loss carry-forward is not major, although there may be some temporary effect as these provisions of the 1986 federal tax law will not be fully phased in until 1991. Other tax facets affecting use of depreciation and use of the leasing fund by qualified plans and Investment Retirement Accounts (IRAs), will also be discussed.

We have included only eight sections for initial concern when reviewing the prospectus. There are other areas that require attention in the review process but our attempt here was to provide a methodology for advisors to quickly sift through the details of the offering statement. As the advisor culls the list of potential leasing investments, further analysis such as we have proposed throughout this book is then required.

20
Getting the Most from Dealer Due Diligence

Leasing fund sponsors, broker/dealer due diligence officers, financial advisors, and investors share the same interest in finding a good deal in which all may profit. But obviously, not all deals are good for everybody. Due diligence is the presumed means in which the securities industry attempts to professionally sort out what is good for the investor in the proposed deal.

However, due diligence approaches can vary widely among the several thousand broker/dealer members of the National Association of Securities Dealers (NASD). "In the final analysis, what constitutes an adequate due diligence investigation is a matter of opinion and varies with each offering," says a NASD-sponsored report on due diligence activities in limited partnerships.

We recognize that leasing fund sponsors, dealers, client-planners, and investors have both mutual and distinct objectives when it comes to reviewing an investment offering. The approach we have taken in this book is that the investment decision must be justified from the investor's point of view. This is only common sense, but this does not mean the process is an adversarial one, pitting sponsor against investor or sales representative against due diligence professional. Very often the appearance of divided loyalties or just cost and time considerations can intrude in the process of reviewing the investment. For example, most financial planners earn commissions from dealers for the sale of limited partnership units while still collecting fees from the client they represent. The due diligence officer may sometimes be subject to indirect pressure from the sales arm of the broker/dealer to approve a particular fund for sale by the dealer's representatives. Very often the broker/dealer will receive compensation directly from the fund sponsor for performing the due diligence on that sponsor's program. These are all sensitive areas in the direct participation investment business. For investment purposes, however, the investor and financial professional needs to be clear about what due diligence is, or is not, and proceed accordingly.

Purpose of Due Diligence

Many broker/dealers consider due diligence to consist of two primary considerations. First, should the investment be sold to the client at all? Second, how will the dealer substantiate the analytical steps to avoid potential liability? There is no prescribed methodology for due diligence of limited partnerships of any kind.

Due Diligence Costs

The cost of due diligence is a significant consideration for smaller dealers. A number of practices have arisen to reduce this dealer cost, and it is important to understand some of these practices because they influence the due diligence process. Here are some ways that dealers seek to reduce the cost of due diligence activities:

- *Pooled dealer investigations.* Perhaps five or six dealers will informally arrange to share due diligence costs in a particular offering in which they are participating

- *Dealer allowances from sponsor.* Subject to NASD guidelines, a broker/dealer will request reimbursement for costs incurred in the dealer's due diligence of the sponsor's offering

- *Research services.* Sponsors will contract with independent experts who will research and prepare a due diligence report. In other cases, broker/dealers will hire subscription services to produce periodic reports on sponsors

- *Relying on captive broker/dealer.* Smaller dealers, particularly, will rely to a lesser or greater extent on the due diligence report prepared by the sponsor's captive broker/dealer affiliate. However, broker/dealers and securities attorneys agree that the dealer should not rely totally on the sponsor's due diligence, because this would fail to satisfy the dealer's own responsibilities.

Coat-tailing. This occurs when a smaller dealer relies on the due diligence of another larger dealer who is participating in the sponsor's offering.

What to Look For

While there are no specific procedures for due diligence activities which have been established by NASD or other industry and government agencies, there is a consensus among due diligence professionals about the basic approaches and techniques that should be in the review process. The financial advisor should be aware of what is involved, and when necessary, should be able to encourage the broker/dealer and sponsor to make sure all the important bases are covered.

Here are some of the practical steps that the due diligence officer should be performing on behalf of affiliated advisors and their investing clients:

Offering Materials. This is just the first step in establishing the big facts of the offering. Unlike many corporate offerings where the underwriter is involved in the preparation of the offering materials, broker/dealers usually receive the limited partnership documentation in more or less final form. As we pointed out in chapter 19, the aim of this part of the due diligence is to weed out the losers and unreasonably exotic offerings. Is there any economic basis for the sponsor's claims and evaluations? If the answer is yes or maybe, then the due diligence investigator proceeds to a more detailed and primary investigation.

Management Review. The due diligence officer needs to kick the tires of the proposed offering. Unlike the financial advisor or investor, it is the job of the due diligence officer to personally investigate the sponsor. This part of the investigation should include extensive interviews with the sponsor's management to gauge management character and capacity.

As part of this management review, the due diligence officer will need to verify the claims made in the offering materials. Often this will take the form of a thorough review of the sponsor's accounting system and equipment management records. Records are audited to determine that claims for lease rates, equipment utilization, and other elements of the leasing operation are verified. In addition, the due diligence officer wants to review how the sponsor has handled the funds of investors in prior programs. Very often, accountants are hired to join the due diligence team on these onsite visits. For leasing funds, independent experts may also be called in by the due diligence officer to assure that the documents of the leasing operation have been fairly kept and that the leasing projections from the sponsor correspond to real market conditions.

As pointed out earlier, the review of sponsor management consists of quantitative and qualitative factors. The due diligence officer will watch for management turnover and will scrutinize the personal character of the sponsor's key management. Many broker/dealers, for instance, will hire private investigators to obtain detailed reports on sponsors with whom they have not yet done business. These background checks will cover items of prior employment, reputation, and possible involvement in litigation.

Bank Checks.   Banks used by prospective sponsors will also be contacted for information, taking care to determine the standing and credibility of the bank itself.

Prior Investor Contacts.   Due diligence officers should also survey a number of investors in prior sponsor funds. This is often a very illuminating part of the investigation where unseen problems can be detected.

Supplier Contacts.   Suppliers of the sponsor can provide useful information on the financial condition of the sponsor. In the case where a sponsor has contracted with an independent lease management company that will handle the fund's assets, a visit to this firm is also required by the members of the due diligence team.

Lessee Checks.   Contacts with lessees of equipment managed directly or indirectly by the sponsor will provide another basis for determining the effectiveness of the sponsor's leasing expertise.

Tax Opinion.   The due diligence officer should verify the tax opinion of the sponsor's offering documents. For example, is the sponsor's tax evaluation based on IRS rulings or the opinion of the sponsor's tax counsel? Due diligence review also needs to determine if the sponsor's tax opinion is based on questions of law or merely a recitation of the discussion without a conclusion.

Mechanics of Offering.   General partner management compensation arrangements should demonstrate mutual identity of interest between sponsor and investor, as we have pointed out in this book. The due diligence officer will want to review matters of compensation, partnership agreements, escrow handling of funds, compliance with regulatory requirements, potential conflicts of interest, and guarantees made by the sponsor.

Checklist of Questions for Due Diligence

The National Association of Securities Dealers (NASD) has illustrated the steps that broker/dealers might take in their due diligence investigation. These questions for the due diligence officer by financial advisors are not intended to be a maximum or minimum level of effort, but they will indicate the sorts of activities that the broker/dealer should be doing.

Did the broker/dealer due diligence officer:

1. Investigate whether the basic economic merits of the proposed undertaking and the results of prior activity have been adequately and meaningfully disclosed?
2. Review applicable partnership agreements for legal adequacy and tax consequences?
3. Perform a physical inspection of properties, plant, and equipment of the sponsor?

4. Review the financial stability, reputation within the industry and other available information on the sponsor's background, qualifications and experience?
5. Examine the program for conflicts, risk factors, proposed activities and financial status?
6. Examine the material records submitted by appraisers, engineers and financial consultants?
7. Examine the items of compensation with an emphasis on disclosure of all forms of compensation?
8. Conduct a study by qualified legal counsel of all tax aspects of the program to determine whether there is a reasonable basis for assuming the benefits are likely to occur?
9. Examine the experience of management and technical staff in operations and in the handling of funds, as well as the management of projects or services offered to the program?

Source: NASD Special Report on Due Diligence. Copies of the entire 73-page report may be obtained by writing the NASD, Corporate Financing Department, 1735 K Street, N.W., Washington, D.C. 20006 or by calling 202-833-7240.

Details

It is the legal and professional responsibility of the broker/dealer's due diligence officer to inspect the details of the prospective fund offering. But as NASD officials point out, there is a great deal of variation in due diligence procedures, and this means the financial advisor, investor, and even sponsor cannot avoid their own responsibilities in the process.

Very often, unfortunately, the process of the due diligence effort comes down to a matter of who pays? Justifiably, broker/dealers want to keep due diligence costs in harmony with the size of the business, but this does not mean it is good business to downplay the concerns of the affiliated advisor or investor.

Likewise, the financial advisor or planner has a fiduciary responsibility to his client. There has been a great deal of discussion within the financial planning industry in recent years about the advisability of accepting any sponsor commissions from the sale of registered securities that they recommend to clients. Some argue that a fee-only basis of financial planner compensation is the only way to avoid the appearance of divided loyalties.

Summary

What we have sought in this book is to provide a functional basis for understanding and evaluating equipment leasing limited partnerships. This understanding is a necessary part of the job played by all parties to the deal: sponsor, broker/dealer, financial advisor, and investor.

The investor must do his or her homework, too. If a broker/dealer approves a leasing fund for sale, that does not mean the investor should buy the fund. Neither does it mean that the financial advisor or dealer should recommend the fund to all investors. The investor is putting up his or her money and relies on the advice of the financial advisor. But this is a choice made by the investor, and it should only be made after the investor has digested and understood the economics and risks associated with the investment.

The financial advisor or investor does not need to be an expert in equipment leasing to be able to effectively judge an investment in a leasing income fund. There is a lot of common sense in the choice. But financial advisors, investors, and others involved in the process need to understand what is involved in the evaluation and choice of a leasing fund. We hope this book assists this community of sponsor, dealer, advisor, and investor in knowing what to look for and how to go about presenting and making an informed investment choice.

IV
Resources

Appendix A
Glossary of Key Equipment Leasing Terms

Accelerated cost recovery system: System in which the Internal Revenue Service has established depreciation deductions.

ACRS: *See* Accelerated cost recovery system.

ADR: *See* Asset depreciation range.

Advance rent: Rent that precedes regular lease term and basic lease rental.

Alternative minimum tax: Separate federal income tax that is imposed when the minimum tax exceeds regular corporate tax.

AMT: *See* Alternative minimum tax.

Asset depreciation range: A method of tax depreciation used before ACRS. It may still be used in instances where alternative minimum tax is applied.

At-risk: Federal tax rules which prohibit individuals and corporations from deducting tax losses beyond the amount at which they are at risk.

Bargain purchase option: Option granted lessee to purchase equipment at end of lease for price substantially below anticipated fair value so that the purchases option appears reasonably assured at the start of the lease.

Broker: Company or individual that arranges lease transaction between lessee and lessor for a fee.

Call: An option to purchase an asset at a set price or in a lease option fund where the fund purchases the right to participate in the residual proceeds of an asset.

Capital lease: A lease that meets the criteria established by the Financial Accounting Standards Board (FASB 13) and which will be treated as a loan for accounting purposes.

Conditional sale lease: A lease that is treated as a conditional sale where the user for tax purposes will be treated as the owner of the asset. Also referred to as lease intended as security, money-over- money lease, and a hire purchase agreement.

Depreciation: Allowance and allocation of the cost of a depleting asset for tax purposes permitted over a period of time.

Direct lease: A nonleveraged lease that meets various criteria under FASB 13.

Discounted cash flow: Future cash flow that has been discounted at a given compound rate to arrive at a present value of the future cash flow.

Equity kicker: A share or right to share in ownership in a company or project as part of making a loan or lease. Can take several forms such as stock, warrants, purchase options, or percentage of future profits.

Fair market rental: Price for sale of asset that can be obtained in an arms-length transaction.

Fixed price option: Lease option where lessee can purchase the equipment for a price predetermined at the onset of the lease.

Floating rate rental: Rental that can vary up or down with changes in prime interest or commercial paper rates.

Full payout lease: A lease whose total cash flows cover the acquisition cost of the equipment, overhead, and an acceptable return on the investment for the lessor.

Full service lease: Lease in which the lessor is obligated to provide for maintenance, repairs, taxes, and insurance of the leased assets. Full-leases are nearly always considered true leases where the lessor will own the equipment at lease end.

Future value: Value of investment after specified period of time and certain interest rate.

Growth funds: Leasing limited partnerships whose aim is to enhance investor capital security through various means, such as reinvestment of a portion of proceeds in new equipment or by selecting high-residual equipment or even used equipment whose economic value diminishes more slowly than other types of equipment or even appreciates over the life of the lease. These funds are usually leveraged with between 20 to 70 percent debt.

Guideline lease: Lease that essentially meets IRS guidelines for a leveraged lease.

Implicit rate of interest in lease: The discount rate of minimum lease payments whose total present value at the start of the lease term is equal to original fair market value at the beginning of lease.

Income Funds: Leasing limited partnerships which aim for high current yields and cash-on-cash distributions that also include a portion of capital returned because of the depleting nature of equipment assets. Limited or zero leverage is used.

Independent lessor: A leasing company investing in leases or in some cases a broker of leases. Term used to distinguish between independent and captive leasing firms and institutional lessors, such as banks.

Hell or high water lease: A term that denotes irrevocable obligation of the lessee to pay rentals for the entire lease term. Derived from provisions common to unconditional lease of ships.

Investment tax credit: Tax credit voided by Tax Reform Act of 1986 for all equipment placed in use after 1985.

Joint ventures: Investment where general partner may enter into arrangements with other leasing partnerships funds or even other entities it controls or manages and where equipment may be bought and sold between the various partnerships or general partner subsidiaries.

Lease: Contractual agreement where one party (lessor) conveys use of assets to another party (lessee) for a specified period and rate.

Lease schedule: A schedule of equipment, rents, and terms under a master lease agreement.

Lease term: Noncancellable period of the lease duration.

Leveraged lease: Lease transaction where lessor acquires the equipment through a combination of equity and debt

Limited partnership: Partnership where one or more parties act as general partners to manage the business and where one or more limited partners contribute capital to the operation, but who are not liable beyond the amount of their contribution. Leasing partnerships may be organized as either private or public offerings where the general partner manages the operation of the partnership.

Master lease: In effect a line of credit that permits lessee to add equipment under predetermined rates and conditions.

Minimum lease payments: All payments that lessee is obligated to make for use of equipment. Includes payments for guaranteed residual values, bargain renewal rents, or purchase options.

Net lease: A lease in which payments to the lessor do not include insurance, maintenance, or other items that are paid separately by the lessee. Sometimes called net-net or even triple-net lease.

Net monthly lease rate: This is the net monthly rental payment expressed as a percentage of original equipment cost. The effective annual lease rate would be the NMLR × 12. The term lease rate is sometimes confused with the implicit interest rate in a lease.

Open-end lease: Refers to lease where the lessee's liability is open ended, because the lessee does not know the extent of liability to the lessor until the equipment is sold. If the sale price is below an agreed residual value, the lessee pays the difference to the lessor; if sale price is above the stated residual value, lessor returns the difference.

Operating lease: Any lease where cash flows during the initial term do not cover the full cost of equipment, financing, and overhead. Usually short-term in nature, operating leases are renewable after stated lease periods under predetermined terms.

Owner participants: Beneficial owners under a trust in which title to the equipment is held by the owner trustee who issues trust certificates to owner participants as evidence of their beneficial interests in the leased property. Method typically used in equipment leasing partnerships to assign beneficial interests to limited partner investors.

Percent specified: In an offering statement, this is the amount of equipment to be purchased that is specified to identified lessees. The higher the amount specified and the creditworthiness of the potential lessees can improve the comfort level of investors.

Percent equipment on lease: Percent of equipment assets under current lease. More reliable figure when substantial amount of equipment has gone-full cycle, i.e., been released or sold. Percent off lease is a measure of idle assets.

Regulation Y: Federal Reserve Board banking regulations in which leasing activities of bank holding companies are described.

Release or renewal rates: Percent of equipment that has been released to a new lessee or renewed by the original lessee. Figure is especially useful in evaluating management of operating leases. Also refers to the net monthly lease rate at which the equipment was released or renewed by a lessee.

Renewal option: Option given the lessee to extend term of initial or base term of lease.

Residual value or residual rate: Estimated economic value of the equipment at the end of the lease term, expressed as a percentage of original equipment cost. Often the key factor in projecting an investor's yield to maturity. The estimated residual must equal at least 20 percent of original equipment, not counting inflation, to qualify as a true lease for income tax purposes.

Residual sharing: Agreement where lessor and third party agrees to share in the residual proceeds of the equipment under lease.

Sales-leaseback: Transaction where party sells equipment to another party and then leases the equipment through the new owner.

Scavenger funds: *See* Venture funds.

Short-term lease: This usually refers to an operating lease.

Single investor lease: This is the same type of lease as direct financing lease.

Termination value: The minimum amount of the lessee's obligation to the lessor in the event that the lessee chooses to terminate lease before expiration of the lease term.

True lease: A term defining types of transactions which qualify as leases under Internal Revenue Service Code.

Vendor leasing: Working agreement between a vendor or manufacturer with a financing source or lessor who leases the equipment to third parties through the sales representatives of the vendor. Often called vendor programs or lease asset servicing.

Venture funds: Limited partnerships that invest primarily in undervalued equipment—new or used—whose residual value is high in relation to the cost of the assets acquired for the fund.

Venture leasing: Equipment leased by lessor to companies in return for both rentals and equity kickers that enhance the long-term return of the lessor. [Also venture leasing funds whose purpose is to engage is such leasing activity.]

Wrap lease: A lease where the lessor obtains rental rates which amortize the investment over a longer period of time than the term of the initial lease. The lessor must release the equipment one or more times to recover his investment.

Appendix B
Equipment Leasing Fund Sponsors

The following list of equipment leasing limited partnership sponsors was derived in part through a survey conducted in July and August 1988. The list is intended only as a representative listing of sponsors of publicly offered programs. No recommendation of these sponsors should be implied by the listing.

Access Leasing Corp.
480 Second Street
Suite 103
San Francisco, CA 94107
Contact: Charles Kremer   Phone:415-896-5805
Years: 1   # Funds: 2 $ Raised: $4 million
Equipment Type: lease options
Average Annual Cash Distributions: N/A

Airlease Ltd.
2988 Campus Drive
San Mateo, CA 94403
Contact: Douglas C. Kay   Phone: 415-574-5729
Years: 2   # Funds: 1 $ Raised: $92 million
Equipment Type: aircraft
Average Annual Cash Distributions: 10-12%

American Finance Group
Exchange Place
Boston, MA 02109
Contact: George Cranmer   Phone: 617-542-1200
Years: 7   # Funds: N/A $ Raised: $127 million
Equipment Type: diversified transportation
Average Annual Cash Distributions: 10-11%

ATEL
160 Samsome, 7th Floor
San Francisco, CA 94104
Contact: Dean Cash/Janice Wong   Phone: 415-989-8800
Years: 8   # Funds: 2 $ Raised: $20 million
Equipment Type: industrial/medical/transportation
Average Annual Cash Distributions: 15%

CAI Securities
2995 Baseline Road
Boulder, CO 80303
Contact: L. Burke Crouse   Phone: 303-442-0100
Years: 5   # Funds: 1 $ Raised: N/A
Equipment Type: computer
Average Annual Cash Distributions: N/A

CIS Corp.
1000 James Street
Syracuse, NY 13217
Contact: Christian Evans   Phone: 315-425-1900
Years: 5   # Funds: N/A $ Raised: $55 million
Equipment Type: transportation
Average Annual Cash Distributions: 10%

CSA Financial
Two Oliver Street
Boston, MA 02109
Contact: J. Frank Keohane   Phone: 617-482-4671
Years: 20   # Funds: 5 $ Raised: $33 million
Equipment Type: computer
Average Annual Cash Distributions: 12%

Datronic Rental Corp.
1642 Colonial Parkway
Inverness, IL 60067
Contact: Edmund Lopinski   Phone: 312-359-6770
Years: 7   # Funds: 1 $ Raised: $8 million
Equipment Type: telecommunications
Average Annual Cash Distributions: N/A

Equitec
7677 Oakport Street
P.O. Box 2470
Oakland, CA 94614
Contact: Jan Nelson   Phone: 800-445-9020
Years: 14   # Funds: N/A $ Raised: $116 million
Equipment Type: computer/venture
Average Annual Cash Distributions: N/A

Fidelity Leasing
250 King of Prussia Road
Radnor, PA 19087
Contact: Jim Frank   Phone: 215-964-7008
Years: 4   # Funds: N/A $ Raised: $70 million
Equipment Type: computer
Average Annual Cash Distributions: 11-14%

Finalco Group Inc.
8200 Greensboro Drive
McLean, VA 22102
Contact: Donna Singh   Phone: 800-346-2526
Years: 5   # Funds: N/A $ Raised: $54 million
Equipment Type: computer
Average Annual Cash Distributions: N/A

ICON Properties, Inc.
One Summit Avenue
White Plains, NY 10606
Contact: Peter D. Beekman   Phone: 914-428-9000
Years: 9   # Funds: 63 $ Raised: $43 million
Equipment Type: diversified
Average Annual Cash Distributions: 15%

IEA Securities
540 Howard Street
San Francisco, CA 94105
Contact: Dennis J. Tietz   Phone: 415-543-7363
Years: 10   # Funds: 12 $ Raised: $130 million
Equipment Type: marine containers
Average Annual Cash Distributions: 12-13%

Integrated Resources
733 Third Avenue
7th Floor
New York, NY 10017
Contact: Jack Estes   Phone: 800-821-5100
Years: 10   # Funds: N/A $ Raised: $490 million
Equipment Type: computer/diversified
Average Annual Cash Distributions: 10-11%

Leastec Asssociates, Inc.
1440 Maria Lane
Walnut Creek, CA 94596
Contact: Lawrence J. Lucas   Phone: 415-938-3443
Years: 10   # Funds: N/A $ Raised: $47 million
Equipment Type: computer
Average Annual Cash Distributions: 11-13%

McDonnell Douglas Capital Fund
5455 Corporate Drive
Suite 210
Troy, MI 48098
Contact: William F. Doran   Phone: 800-444-4911
Years: 7   # Funds: 1 $ Raised: N/A
Equipment Type: computer
Average Annual Cash Distributions: 11-12%

Phoenix Leasing, Inc.
2401 Kerner Boulevard
San Rafael, CA 94901
Contact: Kim Galatolo   Phone: 415-485-4500
Years: 14   # Funds: N/A $ Raised: $490 million
Equipment Type: computer
Average Annual Cash Distributions: N/A

PLM, Inc.
655 Montgomery Street
Suite 1200
San Francisco, CA 94111
Contact: Allen V. Hirsch   Phone: 415-989-1860
Years: 16   # Funds: 86 $ Raised: $577 million
Equipment Type: transportation
Average Annual Cash Distributions: 10%

Polaris Aircraft Leasing
600 Montgomery Street
Third Floor
San Francisco, CA 94111
Contact: Kathleen Walsh   Phone: 415-362-0333
Years: 12   # Funds: N/A $ Raised: $632 million
Equipment Type: aircraft
Average Annual Cash Distributions: 12-13%

R.J. Leasing, Inc.
880 Carillon Parkway
P.O. Box 12749
St. Petersburg, FL 33733
Contact: Michael Cole   Phone: 800-237-4240
Years: 5   # Funds: 4 $ Raised:
Equipment Type: diversified
Average Annual Cash Distributions: N/A

Textainer Capital Corp.
One Market Plaza
Spear St. Tower, Suite 347
San Francisco, CA 94105
Contact: John A. Maccarone   Phone: 800-356-1739
Years: 12   # Funds: 1 $ Raised: $3 million
Equipment Type: marine containers
Average Annual Cash Distributions: 16%

Thomas McKinnon Securities
1 State Street Plaza
32nd Floor
New York, NY 10004
Contact: Tom Lynch   Phone: 212-482-5950
Years: 2   # Funds: N/A $ Raised: $25 million
Equipment Type: computer
Average Annual Cash Distributions: N/A

TLP Leasing Programs Inc.
711 Atlantic Avenue
Boston, MA 02111
Contact: Nicholas Bogard   Phone: 617-482-8000
Years: 6   # Funds: 14 $ Raised: $190 million
Equipment Type: computer/industrial
Average Annual Cash Distributions: 12-20%

Van Arnem Financial Services
870 Bowers
Birmingham, MI 48001
Contact: Harold Van Arnem   Phone: 313-647-3040
Years: 6   # Funds: 1 $ Raised: N/A
Equipment Type: computer
Average Annual Cash Distributions: 20%

Appendix C
Leasing Information Sources

Associations

American Association of Equipment Lessors
1300 North 17th Street
Arlington, VA 22209
703-527-8655

Computer Dealer Lessors Association
1212 Potomac Street, N.W.
Washington, DC 20007
202-333-0102

Institute of Certified Financial Planners
3443 South Galena
Suite 190
Denver, CO 80231
303-751-7600

Institute of Chartered Financial Analysis
P.O. Box 3668
Charlottesville, VA 22903
804-977-6600

International Association for Financial Planning
Two Concourse Parkway
Suite 800
Atlanta, GA 30328
404-395-1605

International Society of Appraisers
P.O. Box 726
Hoffman Estates, IL 60195
312-882-0706

National Venture Capital Association
1655 North Fort Myer Drive
Suite 700
Arlington, VA 22209
703-528-4370

Books, Publications

Equipment Leasing, 3rd ed., Nevitt & Fabozzi, Homewood, IL.: Dow Jones-Irwin, 1987.

Financial Planning (magazine), Two Concourse Parkway, Atlanta, GA 30328. 404-395-1605.

The Handbook of Leasing, Isom & Amembal, New York: Petrocelli Books, 1982.

The Stanger Register, Robert A. Stanger & Co., 1129 Shrewsbury, NJ 07701. 201-389-3600.

INDEX